STIRRING THE MUD

To Mike –
in admiration
and friendship –

Best,
Barbara

Stirring the Mud

On Swamps, Bogs, and Human Imagination

Barbara Hurd

Barbara Hurd
July 14, 2002

BEACON PRESS
BOSTON

Beacon Press
25 Beacon Street
Boston, Massachusetts 02108-2892
www.beacon.org

Beacon Press books
are published under the auspices of
the Unitarian Universalist Association of Congregations.

Printed in the United States of America

05 04 03 02 01 00   8 7 6 5 4 3 2 1

Excerpt from "The Bear," from *Three Books* by Galway Kinnell.
Copyright © 1993 by Galway Kinnell.
Previously published in *Body Rags* (1965, 1966, 1967).
Reprinted by permission of Houghton Mifflin Company.

This book is printed on acid-free paper that meets the uncoated
paper ANSI/NISO specifications for permanence as revised in 1992.

Text design by Preston Thomas
Composition by Wilsted & Taylor Publishing Services

Library of Congress Cataloging-in-Publication Data can be found
on page 146.

For my children, Tara and Adam

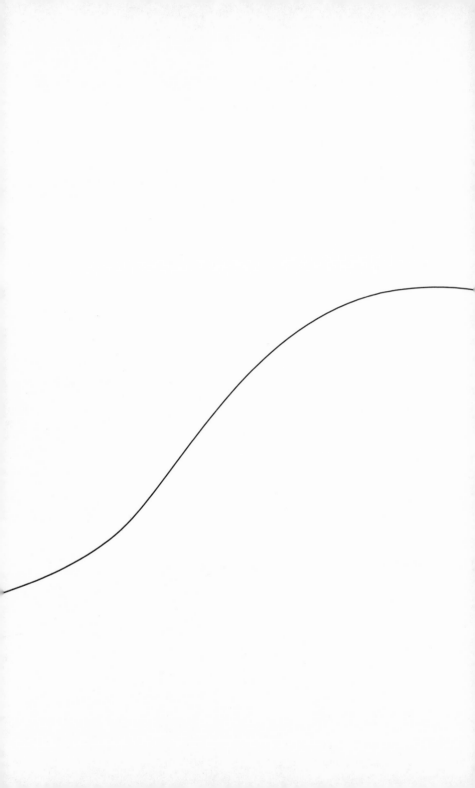

If there were Druids whose temples were the oak groves, my temple is the swamp. —HENRY DAVID THOREAU

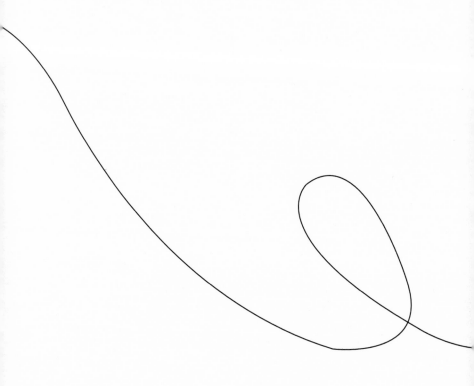

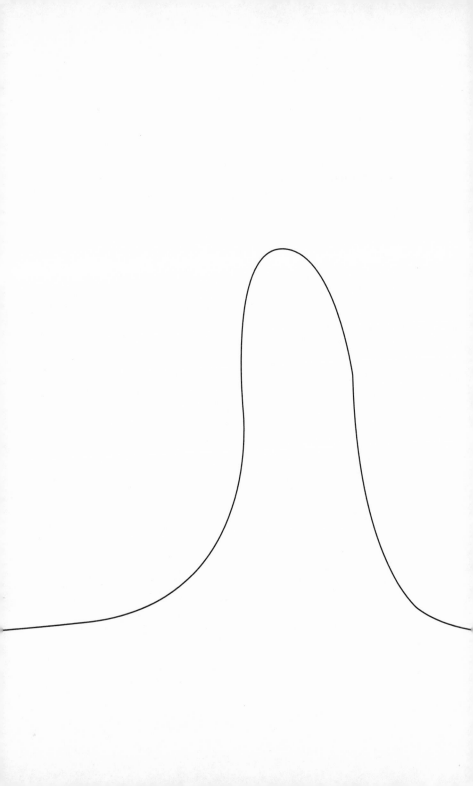

CONTENTS

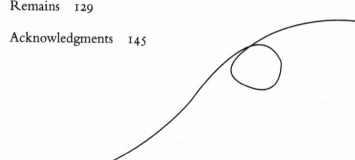

CHAPTER I

Marginalia

> I love a broad margin to my life. . . . Sometimes I sat from sunrise
> til noon . . . in undisturbed solitude and stillness. . . . I grew in
> those seasons like corn in the night.
>
> —HENRY DAVID THOREAU

It is March and I have left the tidy community of Finzel
perched on the ridge of Little Savage Mountain, left its black
roads, its tavern, the Community Fire Hall, and small, dark
houses, each with its plume of smoke rising into the winter
air, turned east and dropped into the white valley of Finzel
Swamp. I have walked out of order and certainty and into the
margins of a land still shadowed by the Arctic.

Finzel Swamp is a relict community, formed thousands of
years ago when the icy tongues of glaciers pushed Canadian
flora and fauna south for hundreds of miles. When the glaciers
receded some ten thousand years ago, most of the boreal plants
and animals migrated slowly back with them. But not here.
Here they stayed, the tamaracks and black calla, in a poorly

drained bowl perched high in the Maryland Appalachians, protected by the even higher ridges on either side. Here in this frozen valley, now owned by the Nature Conservancy, there is no asphalt, no stop sign, no sidewalk, just the wide, white space, pathless, interrupted only by the frozen etchings of alder and black spruce, the scribbled, heart-shaped tracks of deer, the marginalia of some creator who mused for a while on the edge of the page, then dropped the pen and headed north, leaving us to decipher the notations.

I am standing on the frozen surface of the swamp, surrounded by the just-emerging tips of skunk cabbage, a plant that can work on March snows the same way my mug of hot tea does if I set it down on a snow-covered log. The frozen hoods of the skunk cabbage spathe locked in ice just a few inches below the surface begin to breathe in midwinter, and the heat produced by this respiration can actually melt the surrounding snow. Though they say its temperature can be twenty degrees higher than the surrounding air, I have never tried warming my hands over that thick nub of a plant shouldering through the surface. I am too plagued by the memory of my father's decree that we children should weed every last leaf of it out of the streambed that bordered our yard. I hated everything about this chore—wading among fleshy, purple-splotched spathes that rose like hooded bruises, wrapping my small hands around a clump of leaves, large as elephant ears, the fetid smell of mangled green. I know that skunk cabbage has its benign moments—it shelters the nests of warblers, soothes toothaches and whooping cough, and calms the seizures of epileptics, has even, some say, graced dining room tables—but I cannot rid myself of the image of its thick root, like a pale arm plunged into the wet ground, the fist on the buried end tightening its clench around some iron bar of survival each time we tugged. I cannot forget the banks heaped with its yanked and withered leaves, the streambed tidy at last. Or that blurry sense of loss.

Tracks in the untidy edges offer hope, the promise that the page might yield something beyond its justified margins. All my life I have been stumbling over asterisks embedded in texts, slipping out of paragraphs and searching for the footnote, combing the margins for some small note of explanation, the next clue in the treasure hunt, the translation of a word I didn't understand. Always there is the invitation to lift our eyes from the tidy print of our lives and look to the bottom of the page, the end of the chapter, for the source of some idea, for the elaboration of a theory too hastily mentioned. Always there is the chance to trace the path of a creature like the star-nosed mole with its twenty-two pink fingerlike projections blooming on the end of its nose. Crammed with nerves and blood vessels, these extremely sensitive tentacles probe and shimmy through the muck, foraging like an asterisk.

When the German poet Rilke tells us to leave our houses and enter the enormous space outside, surely what he means is to follow the asterisk to the bottom of the page, to drop to our knees in algae, push hands into the fringed and seepy edges into which pieces of our lives have sunk, places where year after year the crust grows thin, too thin, finally, to mask the sense that underneath this unkempt border something else is breathing: the origins of our words, wiser afterthoughts, the whispered asides of the spirit.

Viewed with suspicion and dread by many cultures for thousands of years, wetlands are habitats where the water table has bulged up close to the surface of the land or where poor drainage allows shallow water to linger for months or decades or hundreds of years. Technically, Finzel Swamp is a palustrine wetland—meaning marshy, but not associated with a river or lake. The presence of woody vegetation—trees and shrubs—makes Finzel a swamp. Not far from here, at the other end of the county, lies Cranesville Swamp, also palustrine, but more truly a bog, characterized by evergreen trees and a bog mat of sphagnum moss.

After weeks of cold, Finzel and Cranesville Swamps are both frozen. My boots crunch in the mud as I step between skunk cabbage tips and set off in a northeast direction, where the swamp is bordered by wooded hills. Whether bog or swamp, all wetlands have edges, rich strips where two hands clasp. On the edge, vegetation is always more varied, a mix of mature trees and grassland, or bog mat and shrubs, water lilies and spruce saplings. Browsing creatures and wind-carried seed cross over from one biotic community to another. The young are often raised along these edge zones where, for example, the forest on one side offers shelter and the open fields on the other offer food. These margins are places of transitions and diversity and abundance, one of the most highly trafficked places in the natural world. They are visited not only by creatures who normally inhabit one community or the other and occasionally cross over, but also by creatures known as "edge species," who have specifically adapted to spending their lives in this strip between two communities, which winds, wrinkled and bunched, like the imperfect and wavy seam at the waist of a full-skirted dress.

Humans don't seem to be this kind of edge species, and mostly we're not comfortable here. This margin is, after all, not the continental margin as we know it on summer beaches, where land and sea, in decent intervals, take turns on a tidal edge. Here there is only a constant and languid saturation. It looks as if someone has snapped a photo of a shallow lake and then another of a shrubby, welted, plant-tangled valley and forgotten to advance the film between shots. What you get is a double exposure. You stare at it, trying to separate one photo from the other, assigning this pool of water to the first photo, that clump of grass to the second. Everything is a tad blurry, including yourself as you crawl through both pictures at once.

Maybe our discomfort has something to do with the vulnerability of having an internal skeleton or with our deeply folded brain's hunger for tidy categories. I happened upon an article once by William Hammitt, a professor of wildland recreation, that describes researchers' attempts to figure out how to design boardwalks and trails in wetland areas. They wanted to know what would most appeal to visitors and so they measured their visual reactions to bogs. Either before or after a guided hike through a bog, visitors studied photographs of various bog scenes and then indicated how much they liked the scene in the photograph. What interests me most about this study is the comparatively low ratings visitors gave to photographs of the edges of bogs. Ecologically rich and diverse, that overlap of bog and forest habitats did not appeal to visitors, who found them "unreadable," having no focus and little coherence. This uneasiness is partly about lack of definition.

It reminds me of creative writing students whose first drafts of poems are scribbled messes. "I don't know where this is going; nothing hangs together," they wail, and I urge them to slow down and stay where they're uncomfortable. I tell them "being on edge" is partly what good writing, especially poetry, is all about and I hope they never get used to it. I want them to move out of the places where they feel safe and secure, out of the centers of attention or power or knowledge, out of the center of an ideology, a class. I want them to creep to the edge, nervous and uneasy, to sit as long as they can in that margin between the known and the unknown.

According to Hammitt's research, the least preferred bog scene is the one depicting the open bog mat. In these photos, the bog mat looks like an ordinary field where you might find cows grazing, a couple of deer switching their tails as they raise their heads and watch you, an ordinary field ringed, in the distance, by low hills and dark forest. Yet the people rating the appeal of this scene knew all about deception. They knew any cow who ventured into the mat would sink to its knees, that what is most disorienting about a bog is not only its lack of ground but also its indistinct edges, which make it difficult to find the exact point where you left the forest and sloshed into its quaking belly, the point that, heading home now, you might want to aim for. Hammitt's researchers note this dilemma is easily solved: at the edge of the forest where you enter the bog, you tie a handkerchief. It's an agreement you make with yourself, that no matter how much wandering in tundralike habitat, no matter how disoriented you get keeping your eyes on your boots, making sure they emerge from the muck still laced to your feet, when you're ready to head home, you agree to recognize the bit of cloth you fastened on some spruce branch several hours ago.

It's an agreement you should think twice about, if only because handkerchiefs carry too much history of deception and forgetfulness. Think of Othello, spying Desdemona's handkerchief in Cassio's possession, agreeing yes, this is hers and therefore she must have been with him, her dying, innocent, in his murderous arms. Or Aegeus, waiting on the cliffs to see if the cloth tied to the top of Theseus's mast would be white, signaling his son's safe return from slaying the Minotaur, or black, signaling his death. Theseus, caught up in the revelry of triumphant homecoming, forgot to lower the black flag and haul up the white one, and his father, spying the dark flutter, hurled himself off the cliff. Whole families have been haunted by murder and suicide caused by putting too much significance on the location and color of a bit of cloth. You'd be better off forgetting about fabric. Things in the margins, including humans who wander there, are often on the brink of becoming something else, or someone else, whose memory may not include the significance of old markers.

Under a maple tree where the snow hasn't accumulated, a small hole, maybe two inches across, a tidy entrance. Chipmunk, I think. I picture them down there, half dozing in winter torpor, in their maze of underground tunnels, chambers for napping and eating, and wonder whether they raise their sleepy, tawny heads at the pound of my boots on their ceiling. What goes on in the margins is not always visible. Sometimes, of course, that's because the edges are teeming with what the center does not want to see—the homeless, the abused, the disenfranchised, whatever does not fit the current definitions of normal. We love high drama in this country, mountain peaks and soap operas. They offer us something to tilt our lives toward—that triumph of ascent, that heart-pounding eye-to-eye intensity, that feeling of being wildly alive. Our nature aesthetics sound like movie reviews: We thrill to the surprising twist in the road that reveals the vast panorama, the unexpected waterfall. We canonize beauty that can be framed on the walls, in the camera, or on the postcard.

To love a swamp, however, is to love what is muted and marginal, what exists in the shadows, what shoulders its way out of mud and scurries along the damp edges of what is most commonly praised. And sometimes its invisibility is a blessing. Swamps and bogs are places of transition and wild growth, breeding grounds, experimental labs where organisms and ideas have the luxury of being out of the spotlight, where the imagination can mutate and mate, send tendrils into and out of the water. It should come as no surprise that the most common carnivorous plants are found in wetlands. Here there is room for the thought not fully formed to stretch, roll over, poke its eyes above water. Here is the valley of split-pea soup where what floats like a chunk of ham might lift its meaty head out of the muck and haul itself onto the log next to you, blinking in the sunshine.

Away from the rigor of scrutiny and definition, the need for distinction falls away. Drifting deepens into reverie. You lie half asleep at four A.M. while your life as you know it unravels, plays footsie with some other life. You slip toward the borders of yourself, toward the obscure blooming in the creases, into the forgotten pockets against whose seams your fingers have fretted and chafed until threads finally thin and your fingers plunge into dark, invisible territory of thigh-skin. You drift in a bog as you do in those moments just after sex, everything matted and moist, when you don't know if you and your partner are one body or two. Hours later you crawl out of bed and examine your feet, searching for mud, some smudgy evidence of having traipsed through a place where there is no such thing as ground, where sphagnum moss, curly and limp, holds the lingering twilight the way it holds water. You recall a line of poetry and you know why poets love that white space at the end of a line, how that space invites you to forgo the usual eye-dropping to the left and down to the next line. How it invites you, instead, to launch yourself into that white margin of imagination, where the countryside lies uncharted, wild habitat at the edge of civilized thinking, where the mind is rampant with phrases (*the opposite of stones, the sound of emerald green*) and you feel a certain exhilaration in the tangle and thicket of plant and word, image and water, the mind curling and leaping at the far edge of itself, tiny tendrils of imagination twining their way down stems of waterweeds, cartwheeling across cranberry mats and sundew, never minding the here-and-there unexpected plunge into tea-colored water. At the edge, an open mind leans out so far it brushes the landscape, like the hand of a blind person exploring a patch of grass. This is the edge of a mind foraging through the edge of a landscape. Daddy long-legs and salamanders clamber between your fingers; lichen-covered rocks settle into the folds of your mind.

When I was a child I used to love lying down in the profusion of green that bordered the stream in our backyard after we'd pulled out the skunk cabbage. I'd imagine lying there so still and so long that the fertile fronds of cinnamon fern would drop their spores onto my body. Ideas themselves would become sensuous, so that months later when I rolled my head to one side, I'd feel in my hair the tangle and tug of their woolly stalks.

I scan the hillsides surrounding the swamp, knowing there are bear dens up there. I think about that she-bear, who, last December, lumbered away from the eating and mating mania at the center of most mammals' lives to drift, pregnant and groggy, in the white fields of winter. By now, her fleecy black cubs have emerged, uncurled, and begun to grow. She may still be almost oblivious to them, may only roll over slightly to make her teats more available. Certainly they are invisible to us, hidden in a cave or rock ledge in some isolated spot in the white margins of winter.

Twice I have had the opportunity to head out with folks from the Department of Natural Resources to tag bear cubs. Both times it was March. Both times we bumped over old logging roads in the backs of pickup trucks and hiked over snow-covered ridges to the isolated dens of she-bears snoozing away the last days of hibernation. Both times, a DNR biologist, guided by a radio signal emitted from the bear's collar, crept toward the den, leaned in, and stuck a jabstick loaded with a paralyzing drug into her fur. The drug acts fast and the bear lies immobilized while he gathers her cubs. They chill quickly, yanked by the back of their necks from the warm mound of mother fur and swung out into bitter March air. They are four or five pounds, the size of very small human infants, their fur so soft you cannot help but rub your nose in it. Their eyes are blue and they have no problem looking you in the eye as you take one and open your jacket. They whimper and burrow against your chest as you snap your jacket back up.

Or they scoot up your chest, wanting their stubby snouts against your neck, their heads poking out of jacket neckholes like prairie dogs. I swing between the sheer joy of smelling this wild fur, feeling long claws scrambling against my neck, and guilt. The mother bear, unable to move, watches all of us. I imagine our roles reversed, me lying paralyzed in bed, milk dribbling from my breasts, while creatures from some other world sniff my babies' skin and staple tags into their ears. I know why the DNR does this; I know they are monitoring bear population in this county in an effort to protect them. They are quick, careful, respectful. I am the one needing to make amends. Once when a large male bear ambled out of the woods fifty feet from my house, crossed a thin strip of grass in front of the windows where I stood watching, and lingered awhile among the green beans in my garden, I whispered, *Sure, help yourself.*

Birth is, of course, the ultimate creation. That the she-bear does it while she's half asleep should tell us something about the importance of that twilight zone. Brain specialists say that children's brains are rich in theta waves, and that these waves decrease as we move into adolescence and adulthood. Their most frequent reappearance in adults is during the hypnagogic state, the marginal state in which waking and sleeping overlap, where dreams and reality intermingle. Even our use of the term "twilight" reflects this knowledge—this is the time of twinlights, of the light of day mingling with the light of night, a time rich in dreams and fantasy.

Thomas Edison evidently knew something of the hypnagogic state and used to try to induce it. He would sit in a chair with his arms draped over the armrests, each hand holding a metal object. On the floor below his hands, he positioned two metal pie pans. As he dozed off, his hands relaxed until the metal objects dropped and clattered on the pans. Suddenly awake, he would quickly jot down any ideas that had drifted through his mind in that theta-rich state.

I'm surprised. Not that the hypnagogic state is profuse with half-formed ideas and traces of brilliance, but that Edison's intention to harvest something from that wetland of possibilities didn't dry up the source. How many times I have sat down at my desk, deliberately letting myself drift into some kind of reverie, hoping for a poem, and found only the irresistible desire to curl up on the bed for a quick nap? How many times have I stood running soapy hands over the rims of dinner glasses and had a line of poetry spring unexpectedly through my head? The creative spirit is a shy being, diaphanous. It flits around the edges of things, in the margins, in the sodden ground of swamps where the profusion of growth defies the old image of wasteland. My incursions with the DNR are a kind of trespassing into the margins, a crossing into peripheral land armed with scales and tranquilizers and intentions. Although I am heartened by knowing, up close, the smell of bear fur, I am more glad for the bear with his big feet in my garden, more glad for the slight movement out of the corner of my eye that made me look up from my book that evening to see him standing at the edge of the woods like some soft boulder.

A cold wind rattles through the snags, upright and dead, in the middle of the frozen swamp. I tie a scarf around my neck and zip my jacket. I won't go up into the hills today to poke around for a bear den. There will be better, and safer, chances to see one in summer or late fall. It is, perhaps, the single thread running through mysticism—that you must wait patiently, that to go hunting what is mysterious and life changing with a magnifying glass or jabstick, armed with intent and a sense of your own deserving goodness is futile. Biologists say that wild animals often interpret a head-on stare as an act of aggression. The moment you decide to stare down the periphery, it is no longer periphery. What might have been there either will overwhelm you or, more likely, will sink out of sight, melt back into the trees, retreat to the inaccessible reaches of memory.

The paradox is that to see clearly, you must learn to see obliquely. You must look ahead and, at the same time, widen your peripheral vision so that it extends not just in great arcs around your head, but over the edge, into the margins where the visible and invisible, dreams and reality, land and water, emptiness and profusion mingle. The sublime is like poetry; it will not be caught or chased down. It exists at the edge of things, in the vast margins, like a wild animal. The trick is to learn how to wander there without intention, to float eye-to-eye with fringed orchids, to make yourself available to what lives there, whether it is the rare bittern or a poem or the whole damp and water-lilied world.

The imagination loves freedom first, and then form. And there is an odd kind of freedom in the fringes that comes, in part, from jettisoning our love of function. For centuries, so much in a swamp seemed useless—all this muck and dead trees and algae—and lack of function in our culture means lack of value. *What's it for?* we want to know. *What does it do?* One of the reasons we are now beginning to preserve wetlands, such as Finzel, has, of course, to do with learning their function. We can tick off their benefits on our fingers: they help control flooding or they filter toxic waste, both of which have to do with our physical and economic health.

But what kind of cultural enlightenment will it take for us to freely say that we value this or that because it is beautiful, because it nourishes the imagination, because it is good for the soul? How much longer until we grant ourselves carte blanche to move beyond the neatly printed page into the margins strewn with skunk cabbage, the twilight world of dozing she-bears, to drift in the liminal space between what is and what could be? And after that, what kind of handkerchief knotted at the edge of the familiar could possibly lead you back the same way you came in?

CHAPTER 2

Stirring the Mud

Someone has left a pair of shoes at the edge of Finzel Swamp. Black Converse, canvas, size 12, well worn. They're pointed, toes first, toward the most tangled part of the swamp, as if their owner had walked right up to the water, bent over, untied them, slipped his feet out, and kept going. I kneel and look through the thicket of alder for signs of bent twigs, broken branches, the top of a tussock dimpled by a footprint. It's April, season of mud in Finzel. Everything is draped with the feel of late winter, the snow no longer visible but still almost present on the flattened, dead grasses, in the soggy ground, which, even here, is usually dry. Skunk cabbage is in its full monk stage, the bulbous and mottled hoods poking everywhere through the mud. Hundreds of hunched, tiny Yodas whispering, *Feel the force, Luke. Feel the force.* What is this force that might draw a man out of his senses and out of his shoes, send him barefoot into the mud of the swamp?

What I feel is mud, its allure and its taboo, the child's delight in mud pies, the parent's dismay at soiled clothes and blackened fingernails. They are old and contradictory urges, those calls to play in the mud and to keep our hands clean. I feel it again today, kneeling by the abandoned shoes at the edge of a shallow pool, wondering whether up ahead I'll find his socks and then later his pants. I stretch out my arm, remembering Adam, naked, his hand reaching toward God's on the ceiling of the Sistine Chapel, and extend my long finger into the soft muck of the swamp.

The mud in this pooled part of the swamp is delicate, a puree of thinned chocolate pudding. With my index finger, I scoop a bit into my hand, try rubbing it on my wrist, where it spreads to the edge, drips off my skin. Its top layers are way too soupy for mud cakes. Bending over, I press my palms into its softness; I can barely feel it. How can something be so visible to the eye and so insubstantial to the touch? It's like a stained, warm fog, a cloud of silt or the damp and drifting debris of fine-grained walnut ash.

The shoeless man might have paused here at this pool, lain down, taken a mud bath, as thousands do every year. In places with names like Ein Gedi, they pay money to strip and ease themselves into a tub of mud. The ads tell us that mud rejuvenates. Something about the slight buoyancy mud offers, its traces of pumice, which scour off dead skin cells. You can even buy mud bath products to use in the privacy of your own home. In front of your bathroom mirror, you spread the moor mud on your face and it's supposed to purify your pores, smooth wrinkles, even detoxify underlying tissues. But I wonder whether the success of such products actually has more to do with a grown-up's wish to act young again, some adult justification for smearing and spattering the primitive goop. I consider whether the shoeless man might really be a child with big feet, might have leaned over to make mud pies, to splatter mud onto his nose, his cheekbones, whether he might have lowered his whole face into the mud.

I dip my hands in again, spiral my fingers deeper into the muck. There's a Mongolian myth that says that in the beginning the world was all fluid until a holy being bent down and stirred the water. Unlike Genesis, which says that God separated water from dry land, the Mongols say that the water thickened, gelled, congealed into land. It must have taken a long time, the oceans stirred and swirling, coagulating into continents. And maybe places like Finzel Swamp are just not done yet. Maybe there's a holy being still stirring things here, stirring this layer dawdling between chaos and form. I push my hands in further, into a gunked and shapeless glove that reaches back into the amorphous past. I wiggle my fingers into something pre-body, and suddenly I am nine again, circling the swamp behind our neighborhood, searching for mud-holes.

There were good-sized ones there, three feet or so in diameter, big enough that I could pretend they were skinless bodies I was stepping into, bodies whose organs—squishy heart, burpy stomach, coils of innards—I could wrap around my ankles, a prebirth intimacy I could not have named then, could only feel as a deep comfort, a memory of something I knew only because my little-girl body felt so drawn. Maybe all twins feel this urge to lie down again with the unformed, to touch with stubby fingers some other presence that both yields and resists. My and my sister's lives began in the dark as slick blobs rolling over one another for months and months until time shaped us and sent us squalling, separately, out into the world.

In the neighborhood where my twin and I lived, nine-year-old boys liked to teach nine-year-old girls about things that lived in the swamp, things they could pierce, squash, or capture in jars. Sometimes they'd show us. One day one of them leaned over the mud with a stick, chanting something as he stirred, while another, on his knees, held a jar over the gurgling swirl, and suddenly whatever spirit they'd disturbed flew out of the mud and into the jar, where it burst into flame, a split second of blue bubble and firestorm drawn from the swamp's muddy mouth, a flaring sapphire, a blue being exploding against glass walls.

I took it as proof that God lived in the mud. Everything about Adam and clay, Noah and the flood, it all made sense that day when I realized God's fondness for this primordial, shapeless stuff. This was his home. For weeks I came to sit on the banks, trying to evoke that blue presence, trying to coax that flame from the damp. Even months after I gave up the god-hope, I'd kneel over the mud and stir, watching the bubbles rise from a small mouth in the mud's surface, waiting for the flare, wondering what kind of being had a language composed solely of blue gasping light.

Once, poking around for that light, I found a mass of frogspawn in a small pool and tried to lift it out of the water with a stick. Picture a limp honeycomb, its amber-gold drained to transparency, draped over a stick. Or picture the stars of a galaxy, the Milky Way, for example, in a glop of silver-white gel, swaying two feet over the pond. If babies in utero can hear music, sense their mothers in rocking chairs, what did those tadpoles feel, their embryonic eyes locked in gel, their prenatal world lifted into the bright blue sky, the wide sweep of reed-studded, cotton-tufted swamp spread and glistening below them? And what vision disappeared when I, guilty, lowered them back into the ravel of stem, water, and mud? Here's Blake, damning Newton and his mechanistic view of the world: "his eternal life / Like a dream was obliterated." Which landscape is a dream? Which is our home? The silky soft mud of our origins, the finespun lining of its womb coating our skin, our eyes? Or the sudden gasp of blue space, the spiritual world, as Blake says, materializing all around us?

I learned later that what those boys had stirred to the surface of the swamp and secretly lit with a match was swamp gas, methane, which forms from rotting vegetation. It's a natural phenomenon; methane can even combust spontaneously over marshes. Its mysterious light has, for centuries, given rise to stories of alien beings and bog spirits. But the imagery remains. And in my teens when I discovered poetry and read it for hours, curled in the big chair in a silent living room, I'd see that small muddy mouth again, opening in the mire of my adolescence, its brilliant sky-colored language like lit breath.

Finzel mud is the conglomeration of decayed organic material and the wet residue of continents worn down by millions of years of wind and rain, broken into boulder, rock, pebble, pulverized into silt, and washed downstream. This mud the shoeless man is tramping through was probably mountain at one point, a land mass that rose and fell, was buried by deep inland ocean, that lay under the hand of wind and water for millions of years and finally crumbled, rolled, softened, and splat into these high Appalachian valleys.

I poke my index finger into it and make a tiny canyon, squiggle fast hieroglyphics, triple lines, and crescent moons on its walls, the way prehistoric Native Americans did, 120 meters inside the earth in the gallery of Mud Glyph Cave, Tennessee, its walls adorned with spirals, face sketches, and serpents. Some of this cave art was representational, some not. Some was partially obliterated, some not. Unlike primitive drawings all over the world, however, those Tennessee mud paintings were evidently not part of fertility or hunting rites. In fact, experts suggest that what was important to those thirteenth-century artists wasn't aesthetics or symbols but the ritual of pressing one, two, or three fingers into the soft mud wall, swirling the glyph, and then, in many cases, immediately clubbing or partially smearing the fresh design. What to make of this? Why would anyone crawl so deep into the earth to create and so quickly destroy?

Every line I make in the mud goes instantly soft, the canyon walls drifting to center, the moons gone blurry. When I withdraw my hands, the fine hairs on my arms are etched with wet silt that's gone from form to formless and is on its way back to form again. Mud runs the whole geological gamut, from mountain to silt to sedimentary rock buried below the surface. It's the one substance we can hold in our hands, smear on our faces, that embodies both birth and death. That can blend the wet grains of both creation and destruction into one matter. That is, as Wallace Stevens wrote, the "Centre before we Breathed . . . Venerable, Articulate, and Complete."

Look at it glopping from your hands. Speed the clock up. Pay attention. Yesterday it was an outcropping on a mountain that pebbled into bits under a harsh gasp of wind and sudden dump of water. Last night it pelted into a plain, which rose and fell and rose again, and this morning it lurched down a water chute into this valley where a hundred acres of plants up and died and glommed their decaying matter onto its clayey mush. This evening its silkiness filigrees your hands. Tonight it will plummet below the surface, be crushed by its own weight. Tomorrow it will stiffen into stone.

It's enough to make me want to wear it daily, sackcloth and muddy ashes. To be baptized and buried, to fashion and wreck in its forgiving flesh. I'd crawl, too, into a Tennessee cave if I thought my testament would last for seven centuries.

Muddy swamps birth not only continents, but also frogs and newts and a host of other creatures. They're probably the busiest labor and delivery rooms in the world, their fecund pockets seething with jelly masses and egg cases. This April evening, still hunting the tracks of a shoeless man, I can hear the first male peepers at the far end of the dirt road that bisects Finzel Swamp. Though I've never yet found them, I know from the field guides they're a small, brownish-gray frog with a dark crisscross on their backs, hence their Latin name, *Hyla crucifer.* They've probably just emerged from their winter under bark, and now they're noisy with their familiar, first sound of spring, exuberant with the evening's warmth and prospect of mating. I want to see one, its lust apparent in its darkening brown back, its exaggerated toe pads. I walk quietly and slowly, determined to follow their shrill whistle right to their hiding places in the low branches of waterlogged shrubs. I'm thirty yards down the road when I notice their chorus keeps receding, as if they're backing up as I come down the lane. I listen for frog-plunks in the water, some indication of how they're moving away from me. Nothing. If they're not water-plopping, are they tree-hopping? I sit on the road for fifteen minutes, as motionless as I can. The swamp is silent. And then finally the peepers start up again. I've heard no advancing throng of big-padded thumbs, seen no approaching yellow throat patches, no congregation of beasts bearing crosses on their backs. And yet here they are again, singing not more than thirty feet away. I stand up silently and begin to move again. And again, their chorus recedes, backs up the road as if I've got some invisible force field around me pushing them away. Finally I realize they're not moving at all. My presence doesn't send them leaping over the lily pads. It silences them. The whole road is probably lined with them; they may be hiding not more than four feet away. They're in the alders, the sedges. They've surely been watching me this whole time, holding their throats still as I approach, inflating them after I've gone.

They're too shy to let me see them, and so I decide to play instead and spend the next half hour loping back and forth on the road, using my body the way a conductor does his baton. *Play, strings!* I wave my arms and command the frogs in the east section of the orchestra as I trot backward down the road, away from them. Their high-pitched notes begin again and reverberate over the swamp. *Silence!* I point to the west section, striding toward them, and sure enough, they put down their instruments, wait invisibly for me to disappear. I bound back and forth along the road, Leonard Bernstein springing off and on his stepstool, his small baton bobbing wildly over the reeds, Rachmaninoff's music swelling and subsiding in the throats of tiny frogs.

By sunset, I've had enough, and heaven only knows what's happened to the females who should have been lured here by all that music. Once they do arrive and mate, they'll lay close to a thousand eggs. Each. And they'll attach them to an underwater stem. One by one. Picture a pointillist with a brush, placing one dot at a time on a canvas that will eventually hold thousands. Your face up close to the canvas, you have no idea what you're looking at. Every dot looks discrete. Step back a bit and the dots begin to blur into each other. Back another step and they leak all over the canvas, smear into trees, a woman's parasol, a whole luminous landscape of French gardens. That's how, up close, I imagine those underwater stems: speckled with spring peeper eggs fastened one at a time. Haul a boot out of the mud and step back onto dry land and they're a green, underwater blur. Another step back and the whole swamp breaks out in music and paint.

Luminosity requires a certain distance. Nothing up close looks very precious. In many Native American creation stories, our continent, which they call Turtle Island, began with mud. Some creature—a coot, for example—dives deep into the waters that have flooded the earth and brings back a glob of mud in its beak. Nothing particularly lucid about that. Then the Creator smears it onto the back of a turtle, who gives up its small life and swells into a continent, the mud it carries spreading and hardening and wrinkling into North America. You'd never know, bringing a mud-glob on your fingertip up to your eye, that you're peering at a whole world in the making, ridged and prairied, stippled with rivers, studded with bays.

Frogs, continents—a whole croaking, creaking riffraff born in the swamp. It's no surprise that some of the gods of ancient people plunged in too. One of the stories about Ra, an Egyptian sun god, is that he emerged from the lotus, that his eyes, in fact, still peer from the center of that floating swamp flower. And then there's Horus, another Egyptian sun god, who must have been related to Ra. He's the son of Osiris and Isis, and it's his conception that interests me. Osiris, at this point in the story, has been killed by his evil brother Set, but Isis finds his body and takes him to a swamp, where, evidently, the bawdy shenanigans of swamp life are ample enough to arouse enough of the dead Osiris that Isis can lie down on him and conceive their child. And so Horus is born. Though he became one of the sun deities, he's also known as the god of silence. And Isis, who conceived her son in a swamp, says, years later, "I am that which is, has been, and shall be. My veil no one has lifted."

There is no escaping the universal drama here: Isis lies down in the swamp with the dead, becomes mystery herself, and gives birth to silence. Haven't we all done the same? Slept with the past, courted dead ideas, been born into muck, found ourselves draped in a fine sheen of the worn and silky sediment of surrounding mountains, our hands slicked with the debris of the world? We raise our fingers to our eyes, wipe away mud, lift our heads, and look around. For miles, for continents, for eons, the world seems to battle and blaze. We hunger for its glory. Then, singing and swinging my arms one day, I learn that what I approach in the swamp deflates its throat, withdraws its song. The question is how can we keep crashing about, proclamatory and crass, once we know that so much of the world grows silent in the face of our loutishness? Why don't we spend our whole lives, like Isis and her son, veiled and silent?

I wander away from the silence of the spring peeper chorus, back to the pool with its delicate mud, and take off my shoes. My socks. I'm surrounded by some kind of reeds, hollow and tall. I try to grab onto them, see if they'll steady me as I lower one foot into the ground, which becomes water. They're not firm enough. I let go, sink through the soft-spun mud, down to where I cannot see, cannot feel any bottom, lower, until I touch a thicker ooze that folds around my toes, fills the unevenness of my arches. Down. It is almost unbearable, this sense of no ground, the sight of my calves truncated by mottled mush of the earth. I wiggle my invisible feet.

This is no out-of-sight, out-of-mind phenomenon. I can feel every invisible inch of my leg. No wonder the Puritans hated swamps. Think of it this way: in sex, the more a man disappears inside a woman, the more she feels his presence. But if you're prudish about such things and used to banishing what you don't like, you can't stand a damp and slippery world where the banished keeps growing, where what's buried is so deeply felt. I inch my leg down further. The mud ripples and lifts. The reeds rustle in a slight breeze.

To the Puritans, a swamp had nothing going for itself. Along with most other religions, Puritans couldn't even envision swamps and bogs as testing grounds. Unlike deserts and mountaintops, they were never places to pit one's faith against evil. Forty years in the desert and Moses can lead his people anywhere. Forty days in the wilderness and Christ returns full of the Holy Spirit. But whoever heard of forty days and forty nights mired amid duckweed and cattails? Or of skunk cabbage burning with the voice of God? One could not redeem oneself in the swamp. One could only get sick as black vapors filled the body with disease.

And it wasn't only Puritans who thought so. In another story from Mongolia, God and the Devil, disguised, each took the form of a black goose moving over the primordial waters of the ocean. When God asked the other to fetch some earth from beneath the water so that he could form land, the Devil obliged, but stashed a bit of mud in his mouth, intending to fly off with it and create his own world. His trickery was discovered when he began to choke on what he'd cached in his cheeks. When God made him spit it out, the Mongols say, the Devil's muddy expectorant formed the boggy places of the earth.

If this valley that yields beneath my hands and knees has slobbered from the Devil's mouth, am I supposed to resist its lure of mud and velvet green? Is this some kind of divine temptation I keep giving in to? In Psalms, I read, "I waited patiently for the Lord; . . . He drew me up from the desolate pit, out of the miry bog, and set my feet upon a rock." But the truth is, right or wrong, I'm not looking for rocks here, or rescue. For decades, I have lowered my own feet into mud and, for a few years, my babies' palms, their toes. I'm trying to learn something about tenderness, what Lao Tsu means when he says, "The softest thing in the universe / overcomes the hardest." I'm knee-deep, looking for clues in the mud, drawn again by its softness, how enticing it would be to get down on my hands and knees, let my belly skim through algae as I follow the shoeless man, who, I now understand, has grown silent and veiled, into the thick of it.

The mud of the swamp reminds me of what I daily forget: something is always stirring, nuzzling, and trying to lick us into shape. We are more malleable than we know, more flexible and lithe, still 90 percent water, still pliant enough to be stirred, congealed into something we can only guess at. This notion of our concrete selves—I, you, they—as beings within our rigid armor, it's all a clumsy, brittle scaffolding. Dunk it into the mud here and see what sloughs off. I can barely keep my skin on. Something is moving here, quickening; something is patting us all, pressing into our hearts. Will we harden and resist or relax and respond?

We are not done yet; none of this world is. What does it take to remember this? Mud, blue lights, a pair of abandoned shoes, a bit of music. The Sufis say the notes of the reed flute are the truest expression of longing. Plucked from waterlogged banks, these mud-loving reeds are dried and carved with nine holes, but they recall what they've been. When human breath moves through the hollow, the music is an expression of pure yearning for roots sunk into mud, soft portal we've all come through. I want to lie down in this pool and let the mud cover my body, remember those months before birth with my twin, remember how the formless and soft are kneaded and shaped. I think of the reed and its longing. I think convergence. I think portal. I want to remember in my body the fringes of the Cambrian Ocean where the first green cell leapt from the sea, flopped into swamps, lured by air and the warmth of the sun while still clinging to the silent mud of its origins.

CHAPTER 3
Hyacinth Drift

Cyrus, a Cajun boatman and guide born and raised on the bayous of Louisiana, tells me that an alligator, left undisturbed, will live to be 350 years old. He attributes this potential longevity to the mud and slow water, how the reptiles spend most of their lives in it, coming out only to mate and eat. You can hear the admiration in his voice. We are aboard his small skiff a few miles from New Orleans, wending our way through a maze of bayous, dark bodies of sleeping water. They are fringed with cottonwood flowers, wild iris, and an orange flower I don't recognize, its blossoms like a bustle of burnished sequins. Cyrus points to what he says is a pair of alligator eyes under the overhanging willows. I see only the quivering, narrow-leafed shadows of the trees, dark-stained water, the bright green leaves of water hyacinths. Drifting through this webwork of bayous in the rain, listening to Cyrus's stories, I'm having a hard time knowing what to believe.

Equally disconcerting, I can't even tell whether we've already chugged up this particular channel. I'd stepped on board Cyrus's boat a couple of hours ago, after he agreed, rain or no rain, to take me through this labyrinth that seeps and flows in no discernible patterns. The bayous of southern Louisiana are slow, brackish creeks that cut through thousands of acres of marshland, a much more extensive wetland than what I'm used to in Maryland. They were formed by the centuries-long rovings and digressions of both the ancient Gulf of Mexico and the Mississippi River. The gulf, at times, wandered far inland, soaking the ground, from which it then withdrew. The river, bearing water from the entire midsection of the country, spilled into the mushy, sinking lower Louisiana and split, wandered, cut channels, built up soil, spread in an unmappable, circuitous, still-shifting maze of canals, many of which look exactly alike. It could be we've been down this waterway two or three times already. It could be Cyrus thinks I'm a Yankee fool. Could be he's right.

When it rains in a wetland, this is the question: Can you see with any certainty the line dividing earth and sky? The air on this May afternoon is full of moisture; the land is soaked and rising. Another few hours of downpour and I'll be looking at the world as if through a water glass. Cypress trees will appear as bent, leafy spoons, that clump of moss on the shore like a tentacled sea anemone. Drifting under a willow laden with rain, I can't tell whether what falls from its long sweeping branches is pure rain or liquid leaf. Cyrus flips a cigarette butt into the water and turns the boat into a narrow, almost hidden canal. I gasp. The banks are strewn with spider lilies, white blooms the size of my palm. They look like a child's scribbled sketches of the sun, spiked rays arcing out over the dense green undermat, enough brightness in this rain to make me think of rainbows.

I'm interested in how water changes light and alters vision, whether color deepens in the rain, if the burlappy tufts of hummocks can take on the sheen and softness of satin. If even a bit of water reflects light, if a bowl of water in my kitchen sink throws shimmers on my ceiling, what happens here where the water has been spilled, the land, like a giant sponge, swollen and saturated, the sky lowering itself like a sea blown onto the land? Is the light, reflected everywhere, an almost invisible sheen we're always floating in?

I learned last month that when watercolorists paint, they're after transparency. They want something of the background to come through the color. I love the promise of layers—in people, poems, quilts on the bed—and so I tried it a couple of weeks ago, bought some watercolors, brushes, and paper, and tried to capture a swamp's layers of water and muddy green. Using a technique called wet-in-wet, I dipped my brush into a small jar of water and spread across the bottom of the paper long, sweeping strokes of water. Then I "dropped" paint into the wet paper. This is actually how watercolorists talk: You "drop paint," a dribble of jade green, for instance, like you might drop a blossom into a fountain, a seed into a pond. But I couldn't control what happened next. Color seeped everywhere, followed a path of water on the paper, unrolling a veil of green watered silk, blossoming when it flowed into a puddle. It tinted whatever dampness it found.

I suppose I could have stopped the staining with another brush or a wad of tissue. But there was something serene about the transformation of the paper. It reminded me of those experiments in fourth-grade science when the teacher brings in a jar of pond water and sets it on the windowsill. You stare at the clear water every hour. You can look through it, down into it, see your hand on the other side. Nothing changes. And then one day you look again. There's a pale greenish cast to the liquid. Nobody has added anything. Whatever is staining the water has been in it from the day the teacher brought it in. You look again and again, and though you can't really see anything in particular, you see that something invisible is turning the water green. After a few days you can actually turn the jar and watch a cloud of emerald swirl. Left alone with a bit of light, water, oxygen, and carbon dioxide, algae can grow about anywhere. It scums the water at Finzel Swamp, turns the edges of the bayous velvet, tints the rocks in streambeds. The world is full of invisible single-celled beings, molecules, presences that stain us, tint our air, color our vision, turn a wetland into a maze of watered silk. I let another drop of green paint fall into the water.

With watercolors, you get a layered effect that's different from the layered effect of oil paints, which build color on top of color. With this medium you're layering watery color with light, the white backdrop of the canvas. It's as if the artist wants the color to hang like a sheer curtain, a dyed and patterned veil between the eye and the blank canvas, the way so much of our lives do—patterns of decisions we've made and draped between our identities and the unadorned background of our origins, the tabula rasa, the emptiness we begin with. We make certain friends, choose a school, or not, a job, a mate, or not, whether to have children. We think all the while we're working with solid stuff—steel structures we weld and rivet, gold domes we hoist to the top of our achievements. But the truth is, I think, that we're all fooling around with sable brushes, some dribbles of color, canvas that wobbles under our touch, and a whole lot of water. Water that bends light, distorts size, swells lentils and wood, and hides sunken treasures.

Cyrus says the bayous are full of pirates' booty. He's poled us back out of the spider-lilied, dead-end canal, headed the skiff down another narrow channel with high banks and a canopy of oak. Among the swashbuckling, dagger-in-the-mouth characters, the most well known is Jean Laffite, who in the early 1800s hoarded gold and silver that he loaded into old chests and buried. Many deathbed whispers in the bayous aren't confessions or prayers at all, Cyrus says, but secret directions: *Ten miles south of the bald cypress at the edge of Tigre Lagoon, look for a stand of tupelos. . . .*

Look at the small print of a map through the magnification of a water glass. Look at your fingers wriggling in a water glass. My fingers on a computer or a piano are long and bony. But in a water glass, they swell. Underwater, they're soft, smoother, blowzy almost. It's what I love about Monet: though he worked in oils, his vision of the soft, watery universe seems more true than this parched, arid world we scuttle around in. He saw the world as it was before it dried and hardened; he saw an endless stream of lily pads and harbors. Even his stone supports of the Drawbridge at Amsterdam look like pillars of mist.

Monet surrounded his home with garden ponds of lily pads, and when that wasn't enough, he painted giant murals of them. Some of the canvases were huge—wall-sized—and in 1922 he agreed to exhibit them in the Orangeries of the Tuileries, in two elliptical rooms built to his specification, so that standing anywhere in the room you'd feel yourself submerged in a watery collage of lily pad and sky, long tendrils of weeping willows echoing the submerged stems of lilies. Believing that what was real was not necessarily tangible, he was after things in transition: diaphanous shrubs glowing from within, light moistening into mist, stones ready to evaporate. In his last paintings, he shunned solid forms almost completely: willows, like the one Cyrus and I are floating beneath, become flaming waterfalls. Monet wanted, he said, "to produce an illusion of an endless whole, a wave without horizon, without shore." And human bodies? We're already 90 percent water. I squint at Cyrus, try to see him like an upright puddle shimmering on a bit of board in the middle of a bayou.

Cyrus brings the boat to the bank in a small cove edged by ferns and palmettos, young tupelo trees hung with Spanish moss. He lights a cigarette, says if I want to hike for a while, he'll watch for gators among the half-submerged logs along the bank. I don't know whether he's kidding or not. I step off the boat and wander away from the water into the shrub woods, where I find a small seephole. A seephole is a slightly depressed place in the earth where groundwater rises close to the surface. About twelve feet long, maybe three feet across, this one resembles a giant footprint pressed down an inch or two and filled with grayish-black leaves that look as if they had been charred. Some leaves are less decayed than others; their crinkled surfaces look like the backs of frogs, waiting patiently for bugs. At the heel and ball of the footprint, the water is deeper and clearer than at the arch, and the whole print is ringed with the green of ground pine and mosses. As I stand looking at it, a crow flies overhead. It's a silent crow and I know it's there only because its reflection wavers across the pool at the ball of the foot, disappears into the muck of leaf piles in the arch, reappears in the clearer water of the heel, and vanishes.

If I had dreamed this image of a crow flying through a giant, wet footprint, what would an analyst say? Would she say the crow symbolized death? The footstep an overinflated sense of my journey? Would the bird and the wet impression in the earth compensate somehow for some psychic imbalance of mine? I lean against a locust and watch the seephole, which had held a crow and let it go. Is it possible not to analyze? To resist dragging the image away from its wet earth so it can be dried out and dissected? If I try instead to simply look at the seephole and see again the crow flying through, I still hunger to make something of it. What to do with this mind always ratcheting toward metaphor? If I resist that impulse and look again and again, finally what I feel is the intimacy of a crow flying through a wet place on the ground by my feet. I feel more texture than meaning, more sense of collapsing space than direction. More immediacy than insight. Water begins to seep around my boots; I'm aware of an egret standing nearby, its leg lowered carefully into the shallow water. The grass behind me—sienna brown and wheat-colored—rustles in the breeze; in the sedges, some bird with the constricted click-croak of sore throat calls to its mate. Swamp willow leaves float languorously to the ground. In the bushes, a spider is poised on a narrow leaf. In the moments I can stop the chatter in my mind, the world seems somehow closer. So long as I stand with my rational back turned, my analytical eyes covered, the spider, the egret, even the water table creep toward me.

What greater intimacy is there than to be in silence with others who know your secret presence? I am suddenly less alone, and it has nothing to do with divulgence, those anguished times you huddle with friends and wring your hands over your human frailties. This is an intimacy born of the body—the hundreds of thumping hearts, my own included, the smack of fingers and wings, the murmurs of pink tongues, forked tongues, hinged-at-the-back-of-the-throat tongues, the bassooning of bullfrog, the rasp of winged cries, muddy cries, the thwack of tails and hindfeet. It's not hard to imagine shedding my clothes, my skin grown leathery, my diet of berries and roots, the mind bathed again in wildness of the body.

I'm not an anti-intellectual. I know the satisfaction of a mind in laser mode, the comfortable certainty of inarguable logic. But I know, too, the distance and disdain the intellect, clattering up the steep face of reason, can impose on the body and the landscape and, right now, I'm sweet on the moments of reverie that water induces, the way my mind loosens, grows fluid.

I look through the rain, back toward Cyrus, bent over the water that sleeps, currentless, dotted with duckweed. He's gathered a handful of hyacinths, a bouquet of lavender blossoms. Spanish moss hangs from the cypress like old lace-pewter veils.

The one essential quality of the imagination is that it moves—in wide sweeps, in pinched steps, out to sea, down into the interior. The imagination is polytheistic and polygamous; its groundspring is multiplicity, not singularity. Trying to press a single meaning on its imagery is like asking a river to hold still. It will squirm out of your interpretation, jump its banks, form new rivulets and bayous in its relentless churn toward the open ocean. Image invites image, which suggests mirrors and the ceaseless, duplicitous interplay of one thing and its reflection.

Cyrus, drenched, leans over the water, stagnant, scummed. He's got a fistful of hyacinths. He pinches their bladderlike stems.

Is the whole world a mirage, born not of the heat but the damp?

Any interest in a dream's depth means paying attention to what's inside and below. It's here where the invisible connections lie, drifting, currentless, outside the bright glare of consciousness. Freud likened those invisible connections to mycelium of mushrooms, those long tendrils that live in the moist, fragrant soil. Pull those threads into sunlight and they'll die. Pull the dream out of its bayou bed and into the arid, interpreted world where snakes automatically signify sex, and the dream will dry out. Moistness is what allows an image to slip sideways, to slide past the fixations and into that vast realm where one damp trail dips into a thousand others, the glistening, soaked, uncertain ground of reverie. This is mushy ground we're on, rich, fecund, fertile. It yields, it softens, it winds and circles in a maze of eternal reflections. Images double back on one another, hand out pocket mirrors, a small boat, an array of arcs connected and fractured, a fistful of brushes. What Monet tried to paint was a verb: *shimmer.* To do that, he had to find what's behind the surface that gives back the light. Visitors to his galleries described his mysteriously seductive exhibit as spiritual balm. Monet said trying to depict what's underwater almost drove him crazy.

"Damn stuff," Cyrus mutters, ripping more of the hyacinth out of the water. I step back into the skiff. Prolific, the plant's dark green foliage locks together, forming dense green mats that a boat can't get through, an impenetrable obstacle of flowers, the southern version of ice that can halt a whaler in Hudson Bay. It's the bane of Louisiana watermen. He admits, though, that the plant helps remove toxins from the water and provides shelter for baby shrimp, which, he boasts, he can catch, behead, shell, boil, season, and feed to me in just under eighteen minutes. Shall we? He grins at me.

I ask whether he's seen any more alligators. "Nah," he says, "not yet. Not enough sun. But we'll go look for Oscar." He poles the boat out from under the willow, starts the engine, and heads down the channel. I lean over the gunwale and look into the water.

What is it about water that invites reverie? We know many cultures, like the early ones in southern bayous, had their origins along the food extravaganza of tidal marshes and flooded river valleys. Dependent on the moon sloshing the tides from one side of the world to the other or on spring rains that cause the river to jump its bank, you learn something about seasons and trust. There's no hurrying the tides or the rains, and so your life settles into a rhythm of waiting and working. You adjust your pace to the bayou, its dappled sunlight and Spanish moss, its languid water. So much of the bayou world bends and floats—the land, the white plumes of egrets, lilies, your sense of direction. Surely living by slow water nurtures patience, an appreciation for the quiet. In swamps, you don't hear the jewely jangle of whitewater or the percussion of surf. If you sit still and can hear the water at all, it's more like the water in a well-drenched potted plant. It's a land that, like the poet Roethke, takes its waking slow, a land where one eye opens, ringed with spider lilies and wild iris, while the other eye rolls over under its green lid, heavy with muck and algae, and closes.

You lean over the edge, like Narcissus, and study your own face in the swamp, look for coherence in who you are, the way your face, year in and year out, holds together. Reach out your hand. Tweak your watery cheek. The whole image wavers. In fact, you can make your face change shape. Not just billow out or slither sideways, but zigzag: the upper part of your forehead to the left, your eyebrows to the right. Bent over a pond, I have watched a continent erupt in some tectonic sheer out of the top of my head. Here, a clump of water hyacinth drifts by. Whole chunks of my face disappear. A mess of duckweed, that flat, lentil-sized plant that can turn a pond yellow and green, floats across my reflection, obliterates my cheek. I am dimpled and pocked and shimmering, an illusion idling under a cypress tree.

A swamp is a poor place to go for a steady reflection. This is a broken, shattered place, shards of mirror nestled in the hummocks, jammed between levees. The most you might get is a momentary two-by-three reflection framed in overhanging willows, an image, wavering or still, pierced by arrow arum or water lily, a human being out of whom bloom lushness and wildness, tranquility and tangles, a reflection that dissolves the moment you lean too close, try to disappear into yourself.

Cyrus has spotted another couple of bumps in the water. Alligator eyes under the bayleaf. "Oscar," he says. He reaches into his pockets and tosses a couple of marshmallows into the dark water. Marshmallows?! I look at him. Nothing in the water moves. Cyrus flings a few more. Soon the dark cove is spangled with the bright white of Kraft's marshmallows.

Small puffs of sugar and starch, they bob like unanchored buoys. I lean over and watch one float through the reflection of my face, a small cumulus cloud over my right eye, out my right ear. If Narcissus had been here, he might have drawn back, seen that what he clung to was blotted with small drifting clouds, clumps of air and candy. He might have looked up at last, seen the wood nymphs waiting for him in the woods, avoided so early a death.

I still can't see the alligator. Finally Cyrus takes my head and tilts it, tells me to follow exactly where his finger points, over to the water's edge, and to stare at the space near the roots of the cypress. I stare. The water, barely moving, laps against the bank. A mockingbird sings. The purple blossom of a wild iris drops into the bayou. Another dozen marshmallows drift by. Finally, a small wedge of water under the tree darkens. Watching it is like looking at one of those 3-D, Magic Eye computer designs that hide an image. You practice looking through the glass, trying to see your image reflected. You try looking cross-eyed or blurring your eyes. And then suddenly it's there. The dinosaur, the arch, the heart, whatever had been hidden, emerges in full, three dimensional form, inescapably in front of you exactly where it had been for the full five minutes you'd been staring at it and seeing nothing but myriad squiggles and color.

The alligator is huge, twenty feet, Cyrus says. Nothing moves, not even its eyes. I scan the north side of the cove and come back to it. Still there. I turn to watch the flotilla of marshmallows, headed slowly elsewhere, and come back to it. Still there. It lies like something waterlogged and fastened in the mud. Small ripples of water lap under its eyes. There's a marshmallow a few feet away. The gator doesn't budge. What else don't I see? And what else that I'm looking at is really something else?

For twenty minutes we wait and watch the alligator, which never moves. Cyrus finally poles us away. We drift quietly for a half hour. Conversation dwindles. I become acutely aware of the ceaseless mind-chatter that jangles inside my head. Of all the species, humans seem to be the only ones cursed with almost incessant prattle and gab. We talk to ourselves, each other, into telephones, to televisions, to our dogs. We talk, someone said, because we have mouths. And such talk isn't, of course, always empty. In fact, we have a long history in the West of associating creativity with chatter. We are urged to "talk out the solutions," to associate freely by saying whatever comes to mind, to invent fast and critique later. I often tell my writing students, "Write fast, write lots, never mind that at first it makes no sense."

But according to Chinese wisdom, birds sing, not because they have beaks or mouths, but because first they have silence. Then a song. And finally, the singing. One of the hardest things about learning to sit in meditation is to quiet the mind, to cease the endless blather. You're supposed to accomplish this by counting and concentrating on breathing. Breathe in, count *one*. Breathe out, count *two*. But for me even the numbers are magnets for more words. I silently count *one* and any song with the word "one" in it dances into my head, takes the microphone on center stage: *One is the loneliest number . . . One fine day . . .* And so on, until I'm coming back down the hill of breath, headed toward *two* and lugging a portfolio of music. I need some place to stash all these words and that's what a swamp helps me do. Put me in a room meditating, and songs, like flinders of music, glom onto my head as if it were a magnet. Too many notes. Put me in a swamp and the music begins to leach out of me and settle in the mud. The ground here can hold the most bizarre musings and runs no risk of running out of room.

I hang my head over the edge of the boat again and watch the fragments of my face dimple as the rain resumes and the swamp creeps beneath me. The minute I think I see something about myself, the water ripples. Bits of algae float across my forehead. I have to revise. I think of my twin. In spite of what I know about our origins—we are dizygotic, two-egg twins—if I'm steeped in the lore and mythology of twins, then we are one being sliced in two by Zeus, sent separately into the world with vague memories and this under-the-skin longing for what preceded our birth. I see her face again. She is not me but these are her cheekbones too, and these eyelashes are hers. We tilt our heads and roll our eyes in the exact same way. Are we mirrors of each other? In my hallway at home our portraits hang, painted when we were nine. I pass by them every day and I do not know which is which. Some days I'm the one on the left. Other days, I'm sure I'm on the right. Some days it doesn't matter and some days I want this settled once and for all.

The prophet Tiresias tells Narcissus's mother that he will live a long life *if he doesn't know himself.* This has traditionally been a warning not to fall in love with yourself because such self-love can preclude loving others. But the swamp suggests another reading: you will live a long life if you don't cling to any specific notion of yourself. Narcissus's problem was that he tried to grasp the image of himself, to hold onto it, to cling to it, as if it were solid and graspable, unchanging and real. In a swamp, as in meditation, you begin to glimpse how elusive, how inherently insubstantial, how fleeting our thoughts are, our identities. There is magic in this moist world, in how the mind lets go, slips into sleepy water, circles and nuzzles the banks of palmetto and wild iris, how it seeps across dreams, smears them into the upright world, rots the wood of treasure chests, welcomes the body home.

In a watercolor, when the blue oozing across a wet sky meets the dry paper, the paint forms a hard edge. An ugly, curled ridge they call an oozle. It acts like a barrier. Color can't cross it and neither can water. Neither can insight or vision.

Your reflection in the swamp is never solid. Your face is dabbed by duckweed, chin slimed by algae, forehead pierced by cattails. Here you see your life as a watercolorist's work: a fluid smear of selves laid over and shimmering against a blank background, what Buddhists call *shunyata,* emptiness or basic openness. You hope the artist knows about oozles, can keep the paper wet, feet green, faces half-hidden in the water, vision shifting and kaleidoscopic. This is the self and the body, unknowing, unknowable, baptized in plashiness of melting jade and burnt almond.

Unless we are enlightened beings, our vision is partial, fleeting, mutable, and transformative. To live as if our view is permanent and stable is to cling to what is inherently elusive, to exhaust ourselves trying to cleave to what ripples away, drips off the willows, is pierced by the hollow stems of reeds. We get, at most, a glimpse now and then of the body at home in the soft lap of the earth. We aren't rinsed of our sins in a swamp; we are arrayed in mystery, one foot in a seephole and one in a dream.

The wind has picked up. Cyrus turns the boat and heads back to his camp where, he says, he's got a tame alligator who will pose with me for a photo. He grins at me and points out a wading egret, its white plumes riffling in the breeze. It bends its knee backward, then lowers it into the water. It stares and stares and suddenly stabs its reflection, rippled and wet-feathered beneath it, and lifts a fish into the air.

CHAPTER 4

Refugium

At first that June day I thought I was seeing a small cat doing a weak imitation of an inchworm. It undulated in a strange combination of hunch-and-slink along the edge of Cranesville Swamp. Covered with dark fur, its chin dabbed with white, it reminded me of what theologians say about the life of the personality being horizontal, craving community; and that of the soul, vertical, needing solitude. This mink, going from one alder to another, manages both landscapes, traces with its lustrous back a pattern of swell and subside, evokes an image of Muslims prostrating themselves and standing, Catholics kneeling and rising, pale green inchworms arching and stretching along my forearm. We are gardeners, all of us, our hands broadcasting seeds in the spring, our arms in autumn clutching the harvested wheat. We mingle and retreat, seek company and refuge. We are the tide, the continuous going out and coming in that is the rhythm of our lives.

I have been thinking a lot about refuge, how the swamp has

a long history as hideaway for scoundrels, debtors, enchanted women who guide lost hunters back to firm ground, runaway slaves, and hermits. When I saw the mink, a solitary creature who tolerates other minks only enough to breed and give birth, I had been slogging in Cranesville Swamp, Nature Conservancy land, on the western border of Maryland. I was with a hermit friend who has sold his house, his car, his bike, who is dismantling his identity as an artist living by the edge of the swamp. When he sold his studio, a nearby gallery took his work, including a drawing in which the hair of the goddess's attendants is replaced by a waterfall. You study it and try to puzzle out where their heads end and the waterfall begins. Michael is after an intimacy in his life that has nothing to do with sex. It's a bit disconcerting to sit with a man, his hazel eyes clear, his beard and hair neatly trimmed, who has no concerns about mortgage payments and insurance premiums or how he'd introduce himself at a campground social. Everything I feel about comfort starts to rattle. He tells me, quietly, "I want to live like an animal, close to the earth, self-sufficient, doing as little harm as possible." And ten minutes later: "And I want to live like Christ, close to God, detached, open to the unknown."

We talk for hours on the boardwalk at Cranesville. Michael isn't going into hiding; he's retreating from a path that wasn't headed toward what, for him, is being fully human. He's not sure what that means except a quiet letting go, a deliberate choice to go toward some kind of refuge that nourishes his spirit. All the great spiritual leaders have done it, from Buddha to Christ to Gandhi. They've withdrawn for a few days or weeks to sit in caves and under trees, to wander in deserts, alone, packing as little as possible into their knapsacks.

They're after, I think, some moments of trackless quiet, a chance to blur the footprints, the sense of having been someplace, of having someplace to get to. A chance to see what happens when the past and the future stop tugging on the leash and the present opens like a well.

Those who are fond of retreats—writers, ecstatics, parents with young children—often comment on the silence such time away allows. Silence becomes something present, almost palpable. The task shifts from keeping the world at a safe decibel distance to letting more of the world in. Thomas Aquinas said that beauty arrests motion. He meant, I think, that in the presence of something gorgeous or sublime, we stop our nervous natterings, our foot twitchings and restless tongues. Whatever that fretful hunger is, it seems momentarily filled in the presence of beauty. To Aquinas's wisdom I'd add that silence arrests flight, that in its refuge, the need to flee the chaos of noise diminishes. We let the world creep closer, we drop to our knees, as if to let the heart, like a small animal, get its legs on the ground.

The mink has disappeared into the underbrush. If I had been blindfolded and plunked down in this pocket of cool air and quaking ground, spiked by tamaracks and spruce, home to hermits and minks, and tried to figure out just where I was, I would guess a bog in Canada somewhere, far north of the noise of Quebec and Montreal. And Canada was probably the original home of Cranesville Swamp, which now straddles the Maryland–West Virginia border. We don't think of landscapes on the run, though we know birds fly south in the fall, mountain goats trek up and down the Rocky Mountain passes from season to season, and eel journey from the Sargasso Sea in the middle of the Atlantic Ocean to North America or

Europe in search of fresh waters. But stand back far enough in geologic time and you can watch biomes migrating north and south across the globe as giant glaciers drag and push their icy fingers up and down the Northern Hemisphere. Almost twenty thousand years ago, the last intrusion shoved a wide band of boreal forest south to the mid-Atlantic region. When it withdrew, some ten thousand years later, most of those dark forests withdrew also, reestablishing themselves in Canada while southern deciduous forests reclaimed their usual position in Maryland. But in a few isolated pockets protected in high altitude bowls surrounded by higher ridges, boreal forests hunkered down, sank their damp feet into poorly draining clay and rock, and stayed.

And now they couldn't migrate north if they wanted to, for around them is a hostile world—too warm, too dry, the water flushing too fast through the underground aquifers. Dug up and replanted just a mile to the south, the tamaracks would wither, cranberry and sphagnum would curl and crisp, cotton grass would scorch and wilt in what would feel to them like brutally tropical air. This is an area known as a refugium—a particular ecosystem that cannot survive in surrounding areas.

Historically, refuges are retreats, shelters from danger or distress, and a refugee is one who flees to such shelter for safety. Something in the "outside" world threatens, presses too close, cannot accept the refugee's color or ethnicity or religion or eccentricity, the need for so much water and cool air. Something in the refuge spells protection. If you can hack, float, stagger, climb your way into the jungle, swamp, desert, or mountain, the color of your skin and how you worship won't matter. But something else will. Mohammed in his cave knew this, and Jesus in the desert, the Buddha under the Wisdom Tree. Michael in the swamp does too.

Refuge means a certain amount of quiet, a retreat from what frazzles and buzzes, from what sometimes feels in the mind like the continuous replay of the final minutes of a tied Super Bowl game, bleachers sagging with spectators whooping and jeering about wins and losses, voices hoarse, the players' one-point attention on flattening whatever comes between them and the triumph of a square yard of pigskin flying over the goal line. On an ordinary day, the human ear is bombarded with sound—anything and everything: the whine of a mosquito, the neighbor's lawn mower, the ratchety clock movement, sirens, seagulls, an old dog's snoring, car engines, and the popping roll of tires on hot pavement. Our minds, of course, automatically filter much of this hubbub. But at what cost? What happens to that filtered material? Cleaning the filter in my clothes dryer yields fuzzy bedding of dog hair, threads, shredded kleenex, and, once, a striking black-and-white feather, small and striped, cleaned and surely destined for more than the trash. I run my fingers across the lint trap, gathering the clean down. Scraped and softened linen like this was once used as dressings for wounds—a buffer between raw wound and the barrage of bacteria. Too much buildup of lint, though, and the wound can't breathe, the dryer will catch fire, your house will burn down. Does the human mind work the same way? Are there long screens we need occasionally to pull from our heads, run our fingers up, gathering into a pleated, linty accordion the excesses of noise we haven't processed? Do we need occasionally the silence of refuge for the way it lets our minds breathe a bit more easily?

————

The summer I was twelve, I broke both bones in my right leg. Instead of practicing bull's-eyes at archery camp and swimming laps at the local pool, I read for months. I got out of setting the table, folding laundry, and raking grass. My twin did all the chores while I sat on the screened-in porch and plowed through biographies and mysteries from May until September. When I lifted my head long enough to regain my bearings, it wasn't to wonder what all the other kids were doing that summer; it was to imagine what kind of summer my splintered leg would be having if it had its own ears. I reckoned noises from the outside—clinking of dinner forks, whoops from neighborhood kids playing kick-the-can, the spit of gravel under tires on the shoulder of the road—would have been muffled by all that gauze, the thick white walls. I sat in a chaise lounge trying to visualize my bones tender and traumatized, swathed in gauze and then locked into a white plaster tunnel nothing could enter. I thought of how those slim white bone stilts had for years propelled me down school hallways, across hockey fields, along wooded paths and now lay languid and lazy for three months, lounging inside those padded walls with nothing to do but knit back together.

Maybe it was this experience that later led me to find refuge behind the attic insulation. When I shared a bedroom with my twin in a house in the suburbs outside of Philadelphia, I found a way to unstaple the insulation in the attic, slip between the two-by-fours, and crawl into the space under the eaves, behind the attic's knee wall. It was like crawling into a long, cottony pink tent—quiet and dark, an unlikely hiding place. I felt the way I imagined my healing bones had—hidden in a silent padded world with nothing pressing to do but heal. So long as I could tolerate the itching that the pink fiberglass fired in my arms, I reveled in the silence, the guaranteed lack of interruption. Sometimes I took a book to read or a notebook to scribble in, but often nothing, sitting for hours in the darkness up under the attic eaves. It wasn't that my childhood was full of trauma I needed to escape. My father worked hard and my mother tended to us children; there was always a beloved dog around, sometimes a rabbit, and, for a while, a couple of roosters. We ate dinner together every night, roast beef and mashed potatoes or hamburgers done on the grill; my twin and I fell asleep holding hands across the aisle between our beds, and my father made sure to close the windows when a storm came up in the night. But something in me craved a getaway. From a very young age, I was hungry for the privilege of not being interrupted, for a sanctuary nobody else could enter, for a place where I could retreat and yank those lint screens from my mind.

At the exact midpoint of the *I Ching,* the ancient Taoists provide counsel on the wisdom of retreat. Retreat is imagined here as the creative heavens balanced on a mountain, an image of stillness. Such provisional retreat demonstrates strength, they say, not weakness, which causes flight. Retreat is never meant as escape, a permanent disappearance. In fact, its purpose is restorative; what retreats is strengthened by a conscious decision to rest, to prepare for what's next. Retreat can be a wise pulling back, a temporary withdrawal that prepares one for what the *I Ching* calls the "the turning point," the eventual countermovement and return. At some point, the energy that has been building underground, or under the attic eaves, unseen, in private, turns and surfaces, moves back into the world. This is supposed to be a reversal of the retreat, a bringing back into the larger community the wisdom gained in the quiet of contemplation. The danger, of course, is that the turning point may come and go, unrecognized. The ones in retreat may miss the signal, go on fortifying the walls, flooding the moat, growing their own food inside the compound. Or, as with the 450 or so Seminoles still living in the Everglades, generations of hunters and trappers still gliding their canoes through the saw grass as their ancestors did after fleeing from white men in the 1800s, a forced retreat may become a way of being. What countermovement? What return?

When scientists in the early 1800s first studied the bronzy-red and lippy leaves of the pitcher plant, they noted the way it collects water in its base and speculated that this wetland plant served as a refuge for insects eluding predators. Because the insect can actually crawl up the flared flap and hide in the shadow of the hood, it could remain out of sight of any marauding bird or bat. This theory of early scientists who marveled at such cooperative effort was soon replaced by the realization that while the pitcher plant is designed to look like safe harbor to fleeing insects, it is, instead, a carefully engineered lure and deathtrap. The welcome mat on the flared flap is spiked with hundreds of tiny hairs, all of them aimed downward, like trail markers, and designed to encourage the insect to descend into the pitcher. Once it crawls or slides past these tiny hairs, it slips into the slick, vertical throat of the plant and down into the main body of the pitcher, which is often full of rainwater. The hapless bug then spends the rest of its life, which isn't long, trying to shinny up the sides of the throat, to take off without a solid runway, to keep its exhausted head above water. Eventually, the insect drowns and the plant has its dinner. If the bug was anticipating an eventual return to leafy branches, a summer of night skies and porch lights, it missed the point of return, misjudged the way a trap can disguise itself as retreat.

And who would think of deliberately entering those vast and trackless wastelands and staying there? Longfellow in his famous poem "The Slave in the Dismal Swamp," describes a place "where hardly a human foot could pass / or a human heart would dare," a morass of gloomy fens, strange lights, gigantic mosses. Many a human foot has gone into forbidden territory, but harder than that is to make the heart go too. You stand with one foot on firm land, the other in a canoe. Behind you is light, the expected horizon of your life; in front of you the green overhead hunkers down, crouches over its waters. And you're startled you could even think of putting your body into this lightweight snippet of rolled aluminum and paddling, heart in mouth, toward what the poet O'Reilly branded a "tragedy of nature."

My friend Michael might agree, for he has sold his kayak, one he used to put in by the church at the edge of the swamp and paddle around in, gliding eye-to-eye with skunk cabbage. He wants to be unburdened. For the Buddhists, *taking refuge in the dharma* means cutting the ties, letting go of whatever hand you've been clinging to, whatever boat you've been floating in. It means shedding your armor, letting what's underneath soften, grow squishy and open. It means, as Buddhists say, *not reaching for protection . . . relaxing in the uncertainty of the present moment.* Those monks must have loved a swamp. Sometimes I think their ancient texts must have risen like vapors straight out of the middle of places as wobbly as Cranesville. That they, lifting their robes up around their knees, might have simply looked at where they were wading, said, *Yes, I see,* and written it all down. Surely there is no better place than in a swamp or bog to learn about uncertainty, to notice how we feel when the ground under our feet wobbles, what small boats or dogma we cling to, what all we must let go of when we look down and learn to trust what's holding us now. Something in us gives in to the place, the lines relax, the definitions go mushy, the body limp with this landscape, itself so limp and ill-defined. What paradox that in a groundless refuge what has been tight and willed relaxes until fear begins to dissipate.

Part of the appeal of a refuge may be its isolation. Here nobody can see you still weeping over a lover who hunched off with another some thirty years ago. Nobody notices how you suck in your stomach when someone of the opposite sex struts by. Or how you don't. A refuge is like a locked bathroom door where you can practice the fine art of extending your tongue until you can finally touch the tip of your nose, which you feel free to pick as thoroughly as you want. Nobody's watching; you can do whatever you want.

Consider, for instance, the hermit found in 1975 by a sheriff and his deputies in Florida's Green Swamp. This solitary Asian man had been so overwhelmed by metropolitan chaos, he'd fled to the cypress and black water a few miles from the roller coasters and virtual reality of Disney World and lived off alligators and armadillos. Hiding with white ibis and leopard frogs among wild orange trees, he was dubbed by the few who saw him "Skunk Ape." I like to think he earned this nickname. That in the relative safety of the Green Swamp, he indulged in some childhood fantasies of branch swinging, chest beating, that it was his dark silky hair against a pale back they saw as he scurried away. Nicknames don't always trivialize and they aren't always meant to humiliate. Consciously or not, perhaps the puzzled observers named his most salient characteristics, the ones that needed the tangled and private understory and the mournful cry of night herons in order to surface.

Of course it wasn't always the chanting of prayer or rumors of escape echoing through the refuge. In Cold Spring Swamp in New Jersey during the Revolutionary War, it was the raucous whoops of a bunch of men calling themselves the Refugees, who thought of themselves as British loyalists but who were, in reality, a band of thugs, terrorizing housewives and stagecoach travelers and then hightailing it back to the swamp to gloat over their booty. Scoundrels all of them, they counted on the inaccessibility of their hideout on a small island in the middle of the swamp. Revolutionary War soldier Francis Marion, swatting mosquitoes, made a different and openly partisan use of a swamp: he used Four Holes Swamp of South Carolina to elude the British. Known as the Swamp Fox, Marion and his band of men could disappear into the cypress and stay hidden for weeks. The Narragansett Indians holed up in the Great Swamp of Rhode Island beyond the reach of white men bent on retaliating for Indian raids. Until December of 1675, when the swamp froze over in an early New England cold snap and what had been almost impenetrable to the white men was transformed, overnight, into a smooth array of patios and sidewalks. They simply walked in and what followed was the greatest massacre in Rhode Island history. What had protected the Narragansetts for so long turned suddenly cold and hard and the enemy got in.

For all the reasons that make most people avoid the swamps—poisonous cottonmouths, saw grass so razor sharp it can slit a horse's legs, alligators that can devour a human whole, that sense of the plant-sky bearing down, the need to stay crouched and wary—they make great places of refuge. And if you add to the poison, the sedge swords, the carnivores, the prospect of being lost for decades, it's easy to see why no matter how determined your pursuer is, he often paces at the edge of the swamp, plucking off leeches, and wondering whether plunging into such unmapped and trackless territory is worth it. Of course, the same goes for you. In a canoe, the water closes silently behind you. On land, your footprint in the mud fills and vanishes.

Runaway slaves knew this, hidden in Great Dismal Swamp making shingles for years, and so did the Seminoles, who fled into the Everglades after the white man booted them from their homes in the Okefenokee Swamp of South Georgia. Unwilling to negotiate, surrender, or flee, the Seminoles took advantage of the white man's horror of the infested waters of the Glades. They established villages on hummocky islands in the midst of quagmires, built small canoes that could glide over shallow water, and used the dense vegetation for cover. In pursuit, the U.S. navy in the 1830s sent a Lieutenant Powell, whose men tried pushing and poling their boats, their boots and sticks slurping and sucking in the mud, the vast prairie sea of saw grass closing in on them. When a Lieutenant Mc-Laughlin in Florida tried to succeed where Powell had failed, he led his men into Big Cypress Swamp on the western side of the state, where dense overhead vegetation blocks sunlight and the still water is thick with spinachy trailings. When the men in their big boots stirred the dark water, they kicked up noxious vapors that made them retch. But more disconcerting than that, circuitous streams destroyed their sense of direction. They wandered, retracing and detouring, unable to use the stars as navigational help because the canopy was so thick. Where water was low, they portaged again and again, stumbling over cypress knees and dead stumps, always on the lookout for snakes. Mist rose, steamy and blinding, from the muck, and when it cleared, the men had only the labyrinthine mirrors of black water, the almost impenetrable green walls of Spanish moss and cypress, no way to distinguish "here" from "there." From the top of a pine one of the men might climb, he'd gaze down on a maze of channels, a nightmare of fractals and mirrors, a kaleidoscope of water and thicket that disorients not because it shifts at the far end of your telescope but because it doesn't, and still you don't know where you are. "My Lord God," Thomas Merton wrote, "I have no idea where I am going. I do not see the road ahead of me. I cannot know for certain where it will end."

In the thesaurus, under "disorientation," they list "insanity" first and include "lunacy" and "bedlam," and that charming phrase "not all there." In psychiatric terms, we think of fugue, dissociation, amnesia, confusion, a dream state. But my favorite is from the dictionary, which defines "disorient" as "to turn from the east, as in the altar of a church. Hence to cause one to lose one's bearings." To turn from the east. How curious. If I had to label a swamp's aesthetics and philosophy as primarily eastern or western, I'd say eastern, without question. A swamp is receptive, ambiguous, paradoxical, unassuming. There's no logic here, no duality, no hierarchy. This is a landscape of curry, not Golden Arches. So what does immersion in the swamp have to do with turning a person from the altar of a church? Especially an eastern church?

Try this: Buddhists say that if you meet the Buddha on the road, you mustn't prostrate yourself in front of him, light incense, ring temple bells, count your breaths, or begin chanting. You should kill him. Huh? The point is that any naming, any clinging, can too quickly become dogma. The point is to let go of everything. In a spiritual swamp, there's nothing to hold on to. Everything is fluid, mercurial. You're on a small tussock one minute, chanting *Hail Mary* or *Om Mani Padme Hum*, fingering your rosary or mala, offering dollars or marigolds and rupees. You're basking in some feeling of grace, until you notice that everywhere you turn, the altars keep slipping under the surface, and the next minute there's a copperhead at your ankle and you're fleeing through the sedges, leaving a trail of stirred murk and sludge.

Years ago I volunteered at a state hospital. For a while, my role was to hang around with a kid named Patty, who was maybe thirteen, her face blank and her tongue silent. We did nothing more than walk around the hospital for months. I don't recall that she ever said a word. I used to imagine that inside her mind was a busy port, a large ship unloading its wares, cranes clanking, foghorns out in the harbor moaning, and men on the docks with small carts, hollering and wheeling the cargo to somewhere else, and Patty's job was to not let anyone know about the existence of this secret port. She was like the screening fog in a special effects movie, the blank page that harbors invisible ink. I used to imagine that whatever this secret trading was, it needed a sanctuary; it needed the fog screen that was Patty so it could carry on its business. It wasn't terribly important to me what kind of business this was or whether it was legal. I remember feeling, more than anything, protective of Patty's silence, as if her retreat were more important than whatever handicap it caused for her in her dealings with the rest of the world. I was stupidly romantic: a part of me even envied Patty her ability to use silence to murder every Buddha in the shape of psychiatrist who rounded the corners of her ward, clipboard in hand. I used to imagine she had befriended the dockworkers and sailors, that everyone in that fog-shrouded port trusted one another to keep the secret until the ship had off-loaded whatever its burdensome cargo was, hauled its anchor up, and set out to sea again, lighter, with a lot more air in its holds and engine rooms.

Later, when I studied dissociative reactions in an abnormal psych class, I thought of Patty and of Eve, whose famous multiple personalities remained, for a while, hidden inside her because they did not feel safe in the noise and crush of the outside world. It made perfect sense to me. There was once even a place in Great Britain called the Retreat, not a spa where the wealthy could stroll the grounds beneath their parasols, but a mental hospital, an asylum, where patients' oddities were treated kindly, in the theory that such protective tolerance could keep eccentricity from curdling into illness.

The boardwalk at Cranesville wanders for about a half mile out toward a clump of tamaracks, where it slips under water. No gate, no *This is the end! Turn around!* warning sign. The crossboards simply disappear under the mud and water and, as far as I know, keep heading east. It reminds me of the bridge-tunnel spanning the mouth of the Chesapeake Bay between Cape Charles and Norfolk. From the air, the bridge looks more like a causeway that abruptly halts partway out in the gray waters of the bay, then reappears a mile or two away. It's as if some engineer's calculations were horrifyingly off, but they went ahead and built the thing anyway. On the road, of course, you simply rise and drop as you climb bridges and descend into tunnels. And so this is what I think when I stand at the point where the boardwalk dips below water: I'll just keep walking and soon I'll enter a tunnel, a tube, perhaps, dug out by some kind of shrew and then widened and braced with pressure-treated two-by-fours, and then I'll reemerge into the sunlight and sphagnum a mile or two further into the bog. I think of the *I Ching,* its cheerful coaching: "It furthers one to cross the great water." The ancient Chinese meant, I suppose, that it's important to persevere through danger and uncertainty. It's what allows the possibility of eventual countermovement and return. But who knows if they had this tangled morass in mind?

I inch my way along the disappearing boardwalk. Michael has wandered off. I feel like an old woman alone on an icy ramp; I want handrails and a walker with ice-grippers on its legs. I concentrate on keeping the soles of my sneakers in firm contact with the mud-slicked walkway, but when the water curls around my knees, wood has softened into slime. My foot rummages around, backs up to the last known point of contact, inches forward again, and finds only velvety ooze. I can't tell if the boards simply stop or if they have sunk down under the mud. I can't see anything below my calves. Now what? The *I Ching* urges me on. Joseph Campbell whispers something about the hero's journey and the need to visit the underworld. My mind ratchets from philosophy and metaphor to the not very concrete world oozing around my legs.

Sometimes, Rilke says, a man has to get up from his table and walk. Walk where? Does it matter? Moses and Jesus wandered into the desert. Mohammed hiked up the mountain.

Michael is considering wandering from one coast to the other. *Solvitur ambulando*—the difficulty will be solved by walking. Rousseau knew it, Thoreau, Wordsworth, Nietzsche, and Austen. They walked out into the hills, country paths, and shorelines, philosophical tramps, all of them, seeking some sort of refuge, finding it, some of them, in the walk itself, and some in the desert landscapes stripped of the extraneous where they wrestled with the holy, and others in the muck and ooze of swamplands from Florida to Rhode Island where they holed up in the thick entanglements, the mucky waters, the trackless shallow waters that twist and bend for miles between overhanging cypress.

What countermovement? What return?

I wonder whether Michael worries about his retreat being a one-way street. What if, twenty years from now, he wanders out of the swamps and mountains and finds so much of the world has changed that he cannot even buy a book without access to the Internet, which requires a computer, which he sold when he sold his house, his car, his bike, and his kayak. What if he emerges with a passion for hand-knotted Persian carpets and caviar and no way to make a living? What if he emerges and nothing, absolutely nothing, has changed?

Out of the desert, Jesus emerged, the Devil's temptations strewn and parched over the sands behind him. Out of the wilderness, Moses' people wandered into the Promised Land. Under the Wisdom Tree, the Buddha finally stood and stretched his legs. Out of its cocoon in the pitcher plant, the *Exyria rolandiana* moth unfurls its wings. It had found refuge there weeks ago and reinforced the safety of its retreat by spinning a tight girdle around the neck of the plant's hood. The girdling caused the hood to choke and eventually to flop over the throat, sealing off the pitcher from outside intruders, much like closing the hatch on a boat against threatening seas. Inside, the caterpillar spun its cocoon in a dry haven. Today it emerges, its wings the color of claret, epaulets of saffron.

Does creation begin or end in the refuge of the fringed world? Did God start in a swamp somewhere, making mossy tendrils first, moving on to the mink's eyelashes, clumsy at first with this medium of land and water and then growing more proficient? Did he learn eventually to step out into the world, turning the brush and sweeping it just so, so that by the end of the semester, the broad Pacific was smooth, the prairies even and lush, the South drooping and luxuriant? Or did he begin with the broad strokes? Did he practice first with an airbrush on the vastness of ocean, high sweeps of the Himalayas, the way beginning art students do, stepping back from the easel, trying to get the broad outlines of their subjects, the feel of paint swiped across a mural? And did he then, as he grew more skilled, hunch over the canvas, end up with a miniature brush for the detailed work of wetlands, the fine scrim of sedges around a burnished lily-padded pool he must make appear and disappear with the seasons?

Do we begin or end in refuge? Which is the going out? Which is the coming in?

Standing at the vanishing end of this boardwalk, I think of the water shrew, whose fringed hind toes can actually trap air bubbles that allow him to scamper across the surface of the water—a sort of built-in pontoon system that eliminates any need for him to stand here debating whether this is the beginning or the end of this boardwalk. The mink is hiding. Around the edges of the bog, the solitary white flower of *Coptis groenlandica* rises from its thready golden stem, which runs underground in a vast, lacy interlocking, its juice a balm for canker sores and irritated eyes. And Michael, here again, is knee-deep in the earth, showing me sundew plants, those glistening carnivorous circles the size of thumbtacks that look like the childhood drawings of hundreds of suns, cut out and glittered and strewn across the swamp.

CHAPTER 5

Erased Edges

One of the rarest turtles in North America sits in my left hand, peeing. The spring sun is hot on my shoulders, turtle urine wet in my palm. The toes of my rubber boots have sunk out of sight in a marshy meadow a few miles northeast of Baltimore. Three hours ago I left my home in mountainous western Maryland, forty-five minutes ago I was doing fifty miles an hour in Interstate 95 rush-hour traffic through the city, and now I'm nose to nose with a small creature who first appeared with dinosaurs in the Triassic Period and has changed very little since. The bog turtle in my hand swims for a while in the air, its small flippers rowing uselessly, trying to find some kind of surface to push off from. The orange blotches visible on its neck identify this turtle as *Clemmys muhlenbergii*. Its shell is a mosaic of scarabs, irregularly shaped, polished scales of obsidian and cedar. When I bring it up close to my right eye and peer between the top and bottom of its shell, I can see not only the obvious orange on its neck, but how that vivid color pales deep inside its shell like the embers of a fire in the far reaches of a cave. I like to think it's some kind of signal, a message from 150 million years ago.

My herpetologist friend Jim supervises a research project in this meadow, a project designed to study the home range and movements of these three-to-four-inch-long turtles, creatures threatened by habitat loss, wetland invasion by multiflora roses and loosestrife, and illegal collecting for the European exotic pet trade. During previous visits, he has epoxied and duct-taped to the turtles' shells small transmitters that emit a specific signal. He and his research associates are trying to track them to see how much room and what kind of habitat they require, so that conservation practices can help restore their dwindling population. The biologists are interested in range, eating habits, and nesting requirements. I'm interested in their semiaquatic habits, how they hang between two worlds at once.

Ecologists consider most turtles a successful group of animals, meaning they haven't been wiped out by predators or by an inability to adapt to changing environments. They're reptiles, not amphibians. Amphibians spend part of their life cycle in the water, often with gills, and later, when they develop lungs, move to more permanent residence on land. A kind of part-one, part-two existence. First you're an adolescent, splashing around in the neighborhood pond, and then your body begins to change and you grow legs, move onto land, spend your days sober and dry. The bog turtle, however, is born in bog or swamp or marshy fen and spends its whole life there, burrowing into mud, hauling itself out to bask on logs, back and forth between wet and dry. As if it can't make up its mind and spends its whole life trying them both. Maybe it's this flexibility that's made them one of the creatures that have changed the least over millions of years. Maybe it's the ambiguity of their habits that interests me.

Ambiguity means being susceptible to two different interpretations, indefinite, uncertain. It comes from a Latin word meaning "to wander." And no places are more ambiguous than swamps and bogs. Their identity wanders between solid and liquid, sloshes back and forth over the line between firm and yielding. Irish poet Seamus Heaney, in fact, called the bog a place that "missed its last definition by millions of years." How did such a sloppy place get past the Creator? In Genesis I read that on the second day, God said, "Let the waters under the heavens be gathered together into one place and let the dry land appear." I'm trying to imagine what happened here, whether God meant that decree in some macrocosmic way and didn't much care about the details of little valleys like this. Or whether it's just been too long and God, having turned his attention elsewhere, hasn't noticed how swamps and bogs defy all those grand "Let there be this" and "Let there be that" proclamations.

The day the bog turtle pees in my hand, Jim and his colleagues are searching for nests. It's June, nearing the summer solstice, the longest day of the year. The search for turtles without transmitters begins primitively, Jim's two assistants tottering through the wetland with two long sticks each. Picture a novice skier without skis, trying to get used to walking over uneven ground with a ski pole in each hand. Only these two are punching the ground with these poles, a rhythmic gunk-down-slurp-up lurching through spongy earth. They're waiting for the sound and feel of something solid down there in the mud, something their poles will clunk against—a rock, an old green coke bottle, a turtle's back. One of the assistants, Rick, is the size and shape of a football player, massive shoulders, chest like a stone slab. He's floundering along, wobbling each time he hauls one foot out of the slop, swinging it forward like a mud-draped pillar, lowering it, shifting his weight, sinking in again.

When Rick's pole hits something solid, he whoops, leans down, and grabs a foot-long turtle by the tail. It's not the shy bog turtle but a snapper, and it dangles in midair like an upside-down patient in a straightjacket. Twisting its shelled body, trying to wrench itself free, it does a sudden swing-lunge for the pole Rick clenches in his other hand, snapping its jaws at the wood, neck muscles distended. This is not the turtle we've come looking for, and the contrast between its fury and the bog turtle's shyness reminds me of that optical illusion we used to puzzle over in grade school: If you look at the drawing one way, you see a demure woman's face, her eyes downcast, feathered hat, something soft draped around her neck. Shift your vision just a bit and the hag appears, warty chin, nose like the bent prong of a pitchfork. The drawing is both women at once. The bog holds both turtles at once. When you reach down, work your hands into the mud, what you touch is as likely to rip a chunk off your fingertip as pee in your hand.

I ease the bog turtle back into its muddy tunnel and leave Rick, the snapper still dangling from his hand, to wander the boundary of this swamp, trying to find its edge. I hike its perimeter with a long stick, jabbing it into the muck every ten feet or so. I can get obsessed about stuff like this, wanting to walk, toe-to-heel, on the seam between things. Once I even enrolled in a weeklong seminar to learn how the government delineates wetlands. The government's guide to finding the edge of a swamp is fifty pages long, complete with graphs and soil maps you need a magnifying glass to decipher. We studied obligate hydrophytes, facultative plant life, hydrology, soil samples, and soil maps. We spent hours mucking in the field with spades and buckets and Munsell soil color charts. But a liquid landscape cannot be nailed down with maps and charts, any more than love can be understood as the biochemical action of pheromones.

In this wetland, I plunge my stick in, study the soil I've disturbed, listen to gurgle-slop, figure that if this hole is wet and that one is dry, then the edge of the swamp is somewhere in between. But it isn't. There is, in fact, no line at all. What's between wet and dry land is a broad border, a wavy intermediate zone whose boundaries don't hold still.

Trying to define the edges of a swamp is like trying to put a neatly folded shadow into a dresser drawer. Our efforts to outline these places are desires for tidiness, a wish that nothing undefined lurk around our edges. But the truth is, even human boundaries shift. Some mornings I wake up small and compact. I barrel through those days, teaching, opening mail, grading papers like a self-propelled lawn mower. Put anything on my desk and I'll take care of it immediately. Other days, I feel huge, airy, globular. Someone's mouth is on the bubble wand. I billow out my front door, roll to the garden, into class. Whatever comes my way I envelop—snapdragons, students, the solar eclipse. I can't grade a thing but I can see the shadow a poem makes, where it wants to go. On those days I can live with how the edges of a swamp shift, how its underbelly can sometimes surge in the center and open up a pond. How the pond can disappear and the woods around the perimeter go soggy overnight. I am both high-geared and languid, driven and lazy. And everything in between.

I spent many an afternoon as a child on the stairway from living room to bedrooms in our split-level home. It was a central place in the house, just off the foyer, and I loved to sit there with a blanket over my head—aware of the front door closing, my father's big shoes on the flagstone entryway, the dog's paws, my mother's pointed heels. From this vantage point, like being hunched behind a boulder just off the trail, I could see and hear the traffic but pretend I was invisible. Everyone knew not to bother me here, that I was in one of those half-here, half-elsewhere moods I would know much later as a kind of germination period. Once, my twin sister and I even fashioned our own seedpod by threading an old rope through the four corner grommets of an old tarpaulin and flinging the frayed end over a large limb of a maple in front of the house. We sat cross-legged in the middle of the tarp, pulled on the rope until the four corners rose around us, enclosing us, and the sack began to rise off the ground. We were actually able to hoist ourselves a few feet off the ground this way and dangle there, a khaki-green sack of twins, a pod hanging heavy on the vine, its seeds hidden inside, suspended and swaying in the front lawn of a suburban neighborhood.

At that time, my family lived just a half mile or so from a small pond, which my twin and I could walk to, cutting through woods at the back of our neighborhood. It must have been on someone's property, but no one ever bothered us there. We went simply to see what was happening, to poke our sticks in the muddy edge or listen to spring peepers. One spring I spent weeks there imagining my stick was a giant pencil with a pink rubber eraser on the end. I imagined crouching on the bank of the pond and systematically erasing the edge, pushing the stubby end into the reeds, rubbing back and forth, back and forth, until the tall green lines grew smudged and crumbly, speckled with bits of pink rubber. I'd lean over, take a deep breath, and exhale with the blast of small bellows and pretend I could see the flecks of pond edge and pink debris fly into a bright blue sky as the pond, unrestrained, spilled over my shoes. There was something quite magical to me about all this, the notion that you could change the ground you stood on by erasing some line. Years later when I was first reading Loren Eiseley's work, I happened across this statement: "One exists in a universe convincingly real, where the lines are sharply drawn in black and white. It is only later, if at all, that one realizes the lines were never there in the first place."

The gift of ambiguity is that it stretches us. Makes us less rigid. Nudges us out of the either/or thinking. One morning when I was forty-two, I stood in my bedroom, changing from a sweatshirt to a T-shirt, and suddenly couldn't remember whether my twin or I was older. Was I Baby Girl A or Baby Girl B? From the moment of our birth, in spite of our parents' good intentions, we were "the twins," a unit who shared bedrooms and friends and chores and clothes and good night rituals, a unit others momentarily dissected by asking which of us was older, as if those thirteen minutes were the only distinction between us. So on the midlife morning when I stood in my bedroom and felt those thirteen minutes utterly dissolve, what swept over me was the realization that if I didn't know which one of us was older, if that distinction disappeared, then I might very well be my sister, not me. Looking in a mirror didn't help. I recognized the face, knew this body was the writer's and that other one the designer's; I just felt that somehow it was quite possible that I had momentarily sloshed into her body and she into mine, that this might not be me sitting now on the bathroom floor, the way if you take a stick and dig a channel between puddles in a dirt driveway, the water from each puddle heads toward the other, and there's nothing to stop the exchange of liquid so that in just an instant there's some new, double-bulged body of water, but no recognizable puddle A or puddle B. So. I stayed in this curious state, spilling between the two of us for about an hour that morning.

Nothing miraculous occurred. I didn't emerge knowing my sister's darkest secrets or able at last to pull off the elegant redesign of my living room she would have. What I felt was how completely fluid my notion of myself can be. How totally illusory the lines are with which we define ourselves. I felt a quiet mixture of relief and sadness about all this. Relief at the momentary dropping of iron definition by which we say who we are. Sadness at how hard we labor to "know ourselves," selves that, it seems, are no more fixed than this boggy ground I'm sinking into.

Here's what I love about the in-between: its inherent ambiguity, how it invites a swaying of the imagination, permits a languid hammock swing between two definitions, two identities. The mind, like the body, swings sideways, rises over one bed of possibilities, pauses at the peak, considers, sweeps down and over to the other side. I am one twin, then the other. This

swamp is land first, and then water, land and water, this creature a waddler, now a swimmer. We are shape-shifters, all of
us, liquid mosaics of mutable and transient urges, and we give
ourselves headaches when we pretend otherwise, when we
stiffen ourselves into permanent and separate identities unsul-
lied by the drifting slop, the very real ambiguities of ourselves
and the world.

A television crew arrives after lunch to film Jim's work with
bog turtles. This meadow research site is controversial because
it lies near a proposed bypass, and the state highway adminis-
tration has been working with conservation biologists to protect the habitat. The camera rolls as he pulls on hip waders
again, fastens his headphones on, dials up a certain turtle's frequency. He listens for a moment, then sloshes off through the
wetland. The reporter, in white sneakers, and the cameraman
follow. Behind them, clouds thicken in the west.

A hundred feet or so into the wetland, Jim stops, turning
the receiver a little to the left, then right, the way astronomers
do, their radars scanning the cosmos, searching for intelligent
messages from outer space. Jim is searching for the origin of a
blip-blip that's buried in the mud. Suddenly he stops, kneels,
plunges his arm elbow deep into a soft place between tussocks.
Moments later he pulls up an old bog turtle, twenty-five years,
he guesses, a collage of epoxy and duct tape and shell, all of
it slathered in mud. It, too, tries swimming in the air, flippers
rowing uselessly. The camera zooms in close as the reporter,
her sneakers sinking into brown puddles, points to the turtle's
back, the orange blotches, asks a dozen questions. It feels
weirdly like having a television crew in an operating room

during brain surgery, filming the surgeon pry up the scalp of a patient, probe the medulla, searching for explanations for aberrant behaviors and mysterious voices. I'm touched by her efforts, as if helping people understand who this turtle is, his age, his blaze of orange, will help them understand the need to preserve this wetland. The reporter bends down and peers under the carapace. The turtle in Jim's hand churns his useless legs and recoils his head until Jim finally bends down, wriggles his arm back into the muck, and buries the turtle again.

Isn't this what we all want—to burrow in the mud and still have someone nearby who can tune in to our frequency? Who can find us no matter how deeply we've dug ourselves in?

The present is always ambiguous. We never know whether we're headed in a good direction or straight into disaster. The most we can do is look back occasionally, see where we've been, what patterns we're prone to. One of the standard methods for mapping a bog turtle's meandering patterns is what's known as the thread-trailing method. The researcher attaches a spool of thread to the turtle's shell so that as it moves through mud and sedges, the spool unwinds, leaves a trail of thread behind. The researcher can come back days later and follow the thread to hidden nesting sites. It reminds me of Theseus in the Labyrinth, trailing the thread Ariadne has secretly given him. It's the only way to find your way out, she tells him. Theseus could just as easily have been in a huge swamp, a maze of channels and troughs, where the only way to get yourself out is to see which turns and twists took you in. And in this place, the monster who awaits you could be as ambiguous as the landscape.

It was the Minotaur, of course, that Theseus was trying to

kill, a human with a horned head, the offspring of a queen of Crete who fell in love with a bull. It's a wonder there's not more of the shenanigans of interspecies breeding in the swamp. This is a place conducive to animal-plant breeding, for the bog turtle to lie down with the bur reed, the dragonfly to mate with duckweed. Here whole new beings might evolve—salamanders with skin of rose petals, toothed lilies, turtles who reproduce by blowing seedpods into the wind. The closest thing I've seen so far in any swamp are the meat-eating plants. Sundews, pitcher plants, and other carnivorous plants aren't limited to wetlands, but these part-land, part-water places are home to a number of animal-like flora. Botanists would say, reasonably, that they've simply adapted to the sparse nutrition here. But I like to think, too, there's a camaraderie here, a tolerance for hybrids and mongrels, a kinship among the patrons of an all-night, half-sunken bar for cross-dressers.

Flesh-eating plants hunt in similar ways. I have no idea about the aesthetic tastes of insects, but surely it's no coincidence that sundews and pitcher plants are gorgeous. Sundews nestle in the bog mat like tiny glistening suns. Pitcher plants wave a voluptuous reddish-purple flower. Who wouldn't be drawn? An insect, however, gets caught in the sundew's sticky secretions, in the pitcher plant's cupped leaves, from which there is no escape. Dissolution and decay follow, and the plant has its meal.

Bladderworts also dine on their prisoners. I found them once in a bog on Negro Mountain, about fifteen miles west of Finzel, a bog with more creek than usual, banks of emerald green rice grass, streambeds with the bullet-shaped scat of muskrats. And bladderworts. Floating in languid waters, the plant dangles small bladders on some of its underwater leaves. They look like small balloons or translucent boils or those blisters I love to pop on bubblewrap. Along swims a tiny crustacean, a water flea, a mosquito larva, heedless of the trigger hairs surrounding the bladder's mouth. If it brushes them, the bladder's trapdoor whips open, whisks the creature inside.

Even cross-dressing flora too inhibited to put on an animal mask can flounce around here. A larch tree, for example, looks like a conifer but behaves like a deciduous tree. Beautifully needled, the larches at Cranesville and Finzel Swamps turn a delicate gold in autumn. Sixty-foot-high sculptures of yellowed lace that by December are as bare as nearby maples, the moss at their base littered with inch-long sprinkles.

And if the ambiguity of species cross-dressing is honored in a swamp, it's no wonder the jack-in-the-pulpit's gender-switching is at home here too. It's a trick that might be worth learning. In late summer, you do a quick self-examination of the reserves you've been able to store up for next spring, an assessment you make by checking the size of your underground bulb, known as a corm. A large corm indicates you have enough reserves to come out next spring as a female with two leaves and a flower. But if your corm is small, you just kick back, wait all winter, and come out in the spring as a male with a single leaf. They call it sequential hermaphroditism, a kind of sexual flip-flopping that lets you gauge your own resources before you choose the gender role you want to play during the next season. How sensible.

And how unlikely. We're the culture that values a dependable, separate self. We're not only the ones with the crayons, trying to stay inside the lines; we're the ones who produce those books in the first place, the ones who've drawn the thick black lines. Something about us insists that who we are and how we interact with each other be as straight-lined, demarcated, and geometrical as our buildings, parking lots, and highways.

By late afternoon, the television crew has packed up its equipment, and Rick has long since flung the snapper away from him and backed off as fast as he can, his hip waders slurping and slipping knee-deep in the mud. I have climbed out of its mud-sedgy home and sat down to pull off my boots. Jim has located another bog turtle. As he lifts it gently out of the mud, I think that perhaps the ultimate mystery is not that there are no clear, impenetrable boundaries in the universe but that we can live as if there are. Why the whole apparition holds up I don't know. I lie back on the hillside, rest my head against what I know are zillions of whirring grass molecules, more space than solid. My skull, though, doesn't fall backward into a galaxy of green stars. Instead, a sheer layer of cloud veils the sun, turns the sky a pale yellow behind a drizzle of rain. When, across the valley, the sun flashes through for a second, suddenly everything is shimmer and dew, like some kind of backlit pointillist painting into which someone is blowing a lot of moisture. Even the long-dead trees in the middle of the swamp glisten and flicker. The alders, the sedges, the hummocks, the hillside beyond, everything wavers, minuscule movements made visible by millions of sprinkles of lights. And for an instant I think, *This is how everything really is, quivering, all the time.* What appears solid is actually a rush of millions of molecules whirring in tree trunks, in bark; nothing is still or impenetrable, not even us. I lie by the water, which expands as the sky falls into it, and the whole vision, utterly silent and delicate, vanishes into the inky pool.

We make so much these days about establishing appropriate boundaries, holding our boundaries, the risks of dissolving boundaries, whether it's with lovers, colleagues, students, or friends. Self-help books are full of advice about setting limits, resisting manipulation, saying no. Rightly so. There's much damage incurred from the brutish trampling into someone else's space. If bogs were human, therapists would make a fortune treating their problems with boundaries. Psychologists' waiting rooms would be jammed with jack-in-the-pulpits, sundews, larches, all the swamp creatures who haven't sorted out their eating disorders and gender issues. But the waiting rooms are empty, and left to their own devices, they all seemed to have worked it out anyway. Plants go on eating animals, the larch drops its needles, the jack-in-the-pulpit switches its sex, the borders relax, shift, absorb others. When, by some act of grace, the lines we think are there dissolve, something else appears, something timeless and rich, an intermediate zone, languid and latent, the lushness of something about to be and in no particular hurry to make it happen. The boundary between physical and spiritual melts and we see that one is always infused with the other. And, as in love, there's also much that's both real and mysterious in the tender and conscious dissolution of identities, much richness in this place betwixt and between, in this realm of ambiguity.

In Jim's hand, the bog turtle shrinks its orange neck, disappears inside its carapace. Some primitive fire still glows in the recesses of its shell, millions of years old, reminding me of a world without form and void, before God separated the light from the darkness, me from my twin, land from water, where you can live on both sides at once and you know, lifting one foot and then another, in and out of the bog, that the bog is your body too, that the lines severing one thing from another are chiseled in air, that you can bend down and blow the debris of erased edges into a sky that will blur with shimmer and light.

CHAPTER 6

The Country Below

Walking toward Cranesville Swamp on a cloudy July day, I tell Michael a childhood dream: The car I am driving has in its trunk an art treasure, something wrapped in black velvet. I have been given instructions to drive to the wettest fringes of town, to carry the treasure through twilight muck, to lean over and press it into the trembling ground until the earth re-drapes its covers and buries it completely. *What was it?* he wants to know. I have no idea, but the image of its burial is clear to this day—that lowering of something that could keep for years if need be, rocking and swaying two feet deep in the dappled soddenness of bog. It was the kind of dream you cannot shake off, that clings to the skin. You notice it at the oddest moments, your arm vaguely green as you reach through a patch of morning sun for the Cheerios box on the kitchen table. Or in those moments, barefoot in the garden, when your toes disappear in a profusion of potato plants. When the past you thought you'd left behind coats your mind with a soft fuzz of pleasure or regret.

Even when it seems most impervious, time is porous. The past leaks back through its own channels, floods the present, appears as an object you dreamed of thirty years ago. Michael wants me to search the bottom of the swamp today, to see if my fingers bump against something from the dream. We both know he's kidding, but emerging from forest to stand at the edge of what looks like a firm field, I want my hands probing its unstitched pockets, combing its layers of treasure and debris.

Like most everything from glaciers and meringue to humans and their relationships, from a distance a bog looks solid. From the air over Cranesville Swamp what you see in autumn is plush umber dotted with tufts of cotton grass, acres of nap rubbed the wrong way, the fuzzed yarns of velvet gold. It looks firm enough, as if you could, in an emergency, throttle your engines back, lower the wing flaps and landing gear, and ease your small plane down in this large clearing between forested ridges of western Maryland, bumping and skidding across a runway of dying weeds and hardened mud.

It's an illusion, like the solidity of glaciers. Once in Alaska, I made my way, gingerly, across a glacier, astonished at how hard I had to work to avoid millwells and tunnels, crevasses large enough for people and dogsleds to fall into, rubble and rock fragment, the debris of high country canyons. I thought about John Muir, galloping and yahooing his way across glaciers like a big-pawed puppy skidding over hardwood floors. Wasn't he afraid of falling in? Doesn't intimacy always reveal the pores, the loosely woven, the invitation to go below, the way the bog invites, gurgling and swaying and rearranging itself around your by-now-somersaulted plane, its tousled layers of sphagnum and cranberry rising over your upside-down windshield?

If you let yourself sink, you find yourself in the neighborhood of bog monsters and the swamp lights of aliens. In high school English classes all across the country, we follow Beowulf down into the murky waters of Grendel's lair. We have grown up with the Swamp Thing lurching through gnarled cypress trees, its breath like wind from Hades, with the Creature of the Black Lagoon, with bog elves and flickering lights luring innocent humans to live burials in quaking mires. Even our language is soaked with its doom: we are "bogged down" in too much work, "swamped" by debts, "mired" in triviality. Once I visited an elementary school and had my students writing poems about landscapes. One of them wrote about swamps, about green ooze, about wishing he could fling a bully cousin into the middle of a burpy crypt of slippery slime. When he read his poem to his classmates, they squirmed in their seats and cried *Oh yuck* and reveled in the image of the brute up to his ears in muck, algae dripping from his pimples.

What is evidently worse punishment than being stripped, desert-style, of unnecessary accoutrements, as Moses and his people were, is being immersed in all of them. All the endless variety of bullfrogs, bog orchids, swamp beacons, skunk cabbage. All the sinking, slurping, lumpy conglomeration of mud and plant and water. This is an onslaught on the senses, where even what you stand on is solid one minute and liquid the next.

Michael and I wander down the boardwalk, a thirty-inch-wide series of planks and cracks the water sometimes seeps through. It's what's below the surface that he has tried to imagine in the piece he's titled "Ludovici's Throne." It's a drawing of nearby Muddy Creek Falls. Muddy Creek itself begins as a trickle draining this swamp, flowing south slowly, widening, picking up speed, until five miles from here, it roars over a sixty-foot drop, the highest waterfall in Maryland. In Michael's drawing, at the foot of the falls, he's sketched an underwater grotto temple. In it, two women whose heads are lost in the mist and pummel of the falls are helping a third one with her robes. You cannot tell whether they are helping her dress or undress. Whether she is beginning or ending her day.

When I was a teenager, my father taught me how to sight buoys on Chesapeake Bay, how to squint toward the horizon and find the one vertical pole bisecting the line between water and sky. How your eye on it could mean the difference between running aground and sailing smoothly into some cove for the night. I learned a lot those summers about setting goals and hoisting sails up the mast, a whole vocabulary of right angles and verticality that seems to me utterly incongruous in a bog. Even Michael, six feet tall, and I, five and a half, seem too upright, too conspicuous, in this place where almost everything else spreads sideways, a loosely woven lid over a bowl. Sphagnum moss stretches its vast network of cells, living and dead, out across the acres. It reaches from the edge of the pond in toward the middle. It will someday take over. It creeps like a thick raft, its underbelly always dying, its sun-soaked surface a dense sponge of pale green tentacled stems. The term "quaking bog" comes from this characteristic sponginess—you can actually step onto the sphagnum, jump up and down, and feel the ground sway under your feet. It would be, I suppose, a way to give a chicken like me some idea of surfing—holding the feet steady, keeping knees bent and flexible, riding the waves of sphagnum and hair-cap moss. Instead, keeping my weight firmly on my left foot on the boardwalk, I press my right foot, gingerly, into the soft earth. It yields beneath my boot; the surrounding sponginess seems to rise, curl over my toe, reach for my instep. To get to what's below in a bog, you don't yank the lid off and expose what's underneath. You simply walk into it, feel the cover give way, yourself sinking. I don't do it. I step back onto the boardwalk and watch the size-nine, boot-shaped pool of black water I have left in the bog disappear. I stare and stare. I want not just the overall effect of having stepped in and chickened out, but the exact way the bog responds to both my courage and my fear. A step-one, step-two, buoy-by-buoy chart of transformation. I want to see this clump of bog moss, that strand of sphagnum straighten and stretch, link tentacles with another, fill in the footprint. But all I get are the quick sparkles of sunlight as plant and water rearrange themselves. If I look away, even for five seconds, and then back, I can see change, how the instep and heel have filled in. But if I keep my eyes glued to the footprint, nothing seems to happen.

It is July and we have come looking for what is buried here and have found, instead, a sundew dissolving an ant. The sundew glistens, like the palm of a wet hand ringed with dozens of diamonded fingerstubs. The ant, attracted by the promise of something sweet, had wandered in and gotten its leg stuck in sticky secretions. The sundew's enzymes, acting like a miniature blender, pureed the ant, whose body began to shrink, wrinkling, collapsing into itself like a black leather balloon with a slow leak. Moments before, we had been watching a dragonfly in the final stage of its metamorphosis. Its four wings unfolded like veined and moist cellophane as it inched along the boardwalk, unsteady, dragging its newly unpacked tail like a drunken bride with a too-long train of tulle. St. Philip says that truth comes to this world clothed in images. Are we to undress it? Become costume managers in reverse, hanging veils and black leather in wardrobes, sending the truth naked onto the stage before an audience who yawns at the dreariness of abstractions? What's below in a swamp, in the memories and dreams of the human psyche, is never abstraction. Not only can we not see our way into dissolution and metamorphosis, we can't think our way either. I am as interested in truth as anyone else, but my faith is in imagery, in following the scandalously particular sight of this ant and this dragonfly, in this drama taking place on the floating mat of sphagnum and cranberry.

When I was ten, I loved the drama of scabs on my legs. I scratched mosquito bites until they bled and walked around all summer, lifting the hard crusty edges of scabs, the way I might have lifted manhole covers in a city street. I loved the moistness underneath. I loved imagining my shins dotted with shallow ponds the size of lentils, complete with sedgy fringes and the chorus of spring peepers, the possibility of lowering myself into a labyrinth. We lived, at that time, in a neighborhood whose northern edge abutted a small swamp, dense and murky. I remember that particular swamp only in winter. I remember the icy hummocks we used as hassocks, half sitting, half leaning against them when we bent over to tie our skates on, the still, shallow water solidly frozen and skimmed with white, the swamp edges solid as playground benches. A swamp that to my child's mind had no depth, only white flatness, a slick surface to glide across. But when geese flew north and the ice thinned until blackwater showed through again, the swamp dropped out of my psyche. In my mind, I must have pleated the land there, drawn one side of the neighborhood up against the field on the other side and left the swamp dangling in the fold underneath.

Thoreau would have us unpleat that fabric, draw the swamp up to our front doors, enter it as *sanctum sanctorum*. Those were my days of being a religious scavenger. I checked out churches the way a person does flea markets, browsing the tables of old toasters and chess sets, their almost hidden histories apparent only in the way the toaster wobbles on three legs, in how the rook with its missing turrets looks dog-chewed. I entered churches back then fingering the oak pews, scanning hymnals, waiting to see if it was here that some grace would waft up from the crypts, from the churches' history of trial and blessing. I was sure that Catholic girls wore mantillas on their heads when they went to mass to protect their pageboys from the disarraying blast of holy light. The fact that I sometimes joined them, bareheaded, and emerged with hairdo intact did nothing to dissuade me from that notion. I was, after all, an outsider in their church and figured my hair stayed put because I knew nothing of their concepts of sin or of their rising and kneeling on the swells and storms of Catholic seas. Or because I knew somehow that grace, for me, if it came at all, would come from some richness underfoot.

What I also knew, even then, was the ardor with which they knelt and closed their eyes as something silent and robed-winged brushed by and touched their tongues. I knew it first, not in a church, but in a swamp somewhere in the south where my parents took me the Christmas I was twelve. The canopy of cypress and gum trees arched overhead; altar cloth of moss draped over cypress knees. On the few higher spots grew green-fly orchids, resurrection ferns, and crimson cardinal flowers. Everywhere the cathedral was flooded with the wine of the sacrament, tannin-stained and clean and home to cottonmouths and water moccasins. An honest church, where the spirit might just as easily rise from below and sink its fangs into your leg as stream down through glass-stained windows, where what is holy only increases the appetite. It is a clever trick. You are going along living what you think is your life. Something drifts by and enters your body, gets in through the holes it bores in your skin or through your eyes, or maybe it tracks a hair shaft down to the pale softness of skull-flesh, follows the root on in. And you know, even as you open your mouth, as you open whatever you can to feed, as you fill your days with bog-walks and poems, that this is a hunger that will never be filled.

Michael and I walk all afternoon, back and forth on the boardwalk, skirting and crossing the bog edge, dipping into and out of the red plush of rugosa sphagnum. A man I know, a wetlands expert, once sank to his chest in a bog more loosely woven than this one, sank until his toes were five feet under, his heart nestled among the green shoots of cotton grass in a place known as Hammel's Glade. He said it was good, good to stand there with the earth up to his shoulders, sepia pools and sedges drifting in waves. Thoreau would have loved him, both of them at home in the swamps, both aware that in between the big events, the graduations, weddings, births, and deaths, lies a damp profusion of chaos and contentment. Thoreau says, "I derive more of my subsistence from the swamps which surround my native town than from the cultivated gardens in the village." Perhaps it is, as Thoreau says, the tenderness of swamps that draws us. Here are places in the earth you can enter without backhoe and chisels and dynamite, without ropes and helmets and lanterns. All it takes is a step off the edge, the willingness to imagine being buried alive, which is how the wetlands man described it, standing in Hammel's Glade while the bog floated its beds under his chin. And that's the rub. Anticipating death is hard enough, but how to go at it in slow motion, immersed in the decay of last century's plant life with nothing to do but chronicle the way one's bones become almost visible beneath flesh?

The man got out, of course, had lunch somewhere, went home. Not everyone does. Bogs are famous burial grounds. There are stories in Ireland, in Germany and Denmark and England, of hundreds of men, women, and children buried in bogs, some of them lured into the misty muck by flickering lights, by bog elves, some of them mutilated and sacrificed, minus their ears, lips, the skin torn off their backs. The highly acidic water in a bog means the usual microorganisms that decompose a body are all but absent. Add in the very cold water and what you have are ideal conditions for preservation. In 1450, German peasants found the upright body of a man hundreds of years old buried to his neck in a bog. Concerned about a proper interment, the peasants went to the local priest, who forbade his burial in the churchyard. The reason? The priest believed the man had been lured into the mire by bog elves. Evidently anyone susceptible to such spirits wasn't worthy of the sacraments.

But maybe there's something else here. Maybe the priest saw the man as someone who had stood too long in the doorway between two worlds. Who knows what his death was like? Perhaps he fell in, got his feet stuck, then his thighs, found that wriggling only made matters worse. Perhaps he stood there in the bog for weeks, contemplating his death. I heard a story once of a husband and wife hopelessly lost in a cave. After days had passed and they had given up hope of rescue, they began to confide in each other as they had never done. They revealed extramarital affairs, the disdain each felt for the other's naïvete, impatience with the way one left tea bags on the counter, how the other liked his left foot to stick out of the covers at night. On and on they went, unwrapping secrets, lifting layers off their life together, until they lay weak and spent on the damp cave floor in an intimacy they had never known.

Of course they were rescued. Hauled out of the labyrinth and returned to their kitchen, where they could no longer stand the sight of each other. Knowing more than they could bear, they divorced, went their separate ways. Perhaps the priest feared what the bog man had learned during his weeks of dying and didn't want such knowledge in the ground outside his church.

Burial in unconsecrated ground was thought to prevent hauntings. In eleventh-century Germany, a woman who died in childbirth was sometimes buried in a bog so that she couldn't return to the world of the living and drag her surviving child back to the grave with her. It's a quirky solution, given the mother's body might last for hundreds of years in a bog, far longer than the child who grows up and dies with a more traditional burial. There is a story in Vermont about a hollow tree at the edge of a swamp and a coon being chased by a young boy's dog. The coon scoots through the dead tree; the dog, fatter, follows and gets himself wedged inside. Years later, a farmer comes along with a chainsaw, drags logs out for his sugar camp, and loads them on the back of his pickup truck. By happenstance, the dog's former master, now a grown man, is in a car following the truck down the road. He finds himself staring at the face of his lost, long-dead dog, framed in the hollow of a log.

Things decay slowly here. What is down there may reappear, bounding over dirt roads in the back of a pickup, combing the German villages for a child. Some cultures believe that when you die, your doppelgänger appears, your opposite, your shadow. It stands there with you at the place where your soul departs from this world. If in a swamp you take your dying slow, then everywhere here must be half-formed doppelgängers, stuck between worlds, restless and roaming through muck, leaning on the giant leaves of skunk cabbage, drumming their fingers on the green pads of lilies, waiting for you to get on with it. If it's a long wait, perhaps they pass the time by amusing themselves. On the peninsula of Djursland in Denmark is an ancient cauldron bog called Huldre Fen. A *huldre* is a fairy who lures wanderers into the fen, captivates them with her dance and song, bewitches them until they forget all else, much like the sirens of Ulysses's day. It beats skidding crockpots across kitchen counters or jiggling the bed in the middle of the night, the way modern poltergeists do, bored by the interminable wait.

There are other risks with bog burials, notably that chances are you won't be found. Most of the hundred and fifty or so bog bodies we know of were discovered by peat cutters who just happened to look down in time to see a foot or a head moments before their spades and machines cut into soft ground.

Imagine how many more didn't look down. There must be thousands of bodies entombed in peat across England that have never been unearthed. And never will, now that the peat-cutting machines have passed over, now that the peat has been bagged and sold and spread over the roots of innumerable luxuriant English gardens.

We like our burials satin-wrapped and coffin-clad. The earth kept at a respectable distance. Too much intimacy and it seems we're all afraid. I have a cracked crock that belonged to my grandmother. When I run my fingers over it, I try to imagine her fingers, bony and gnarled from work on the farm, hauling water from the well, twisting clothes through the wringer, her fingers lifting this crock, maybe filling it with daffodils, setting it on a table before dinner. I'm after those moments when I can't tell whose fingers these are, when the difference between her hand on the big scoop she kept by the well and mine on the faucet in my kitchen is a matter of tilting the surface. Loren Eiseley says the door to the past swings open. It's a one-way street and you can only go backward. But sometimes the playing field tips. The past sloshes into the present, floods the ground you stand on.

Once, lying in bed and looking at an old photograph of myself, I knew not only my face, the dress, but just for a moment, how I had felt, exactly, at that age when my father would appear in the middle of the night, closing bedroom windows in a storm, drawing the bedspread up under my chin. How that room of ivory walls and gingham curtains was suddenly here, and I stretched my feet under the covers as far down as my knees now reach. And then it was gone, that moment, in a sudden displacement, as if the past had bulged up through the ground and sunk again, and I knew in the aftershock that the past is still alive, still everywhere around, separated from this moment by a skim of amnesia. It isn't all we have—this present where we live our whole lives, this tiny dribble of time pushed over the edge. All it takes is a slight wobble of the field for land and water to start sliding into one another, green and brown and fluid swallowed in fold after fold of water and moss and mud, the whole place a sodden mirror, the reflections vaguely familiar. Why wouldn't we be afraid?

When Tollund Man was unearthed in Jutland in 1950, one of the men lifting the body and knocking off chunks of surrounding peat looked at the well-preserved face, had a heart attack and died. Tollund Man's chin is stubbled with whiskers, his eyes closed, lips pressed gently together in an almost tranquil expression. He lived over two thousand years ago, but in the photographs he looks like any number of men I know after a week of camping. His final meal of willow herb seeds, black bindwood, and mustard was still evident. Surely the past lumbers just behind us, or just below. What separates us from the dead and dying can be measured in the seconds it takes to drop through a skim of algae. Below us, the swamp gurgles, rolls over; the bog sways, its bulges and sighs visible from the boardwalk.

It is a truism in many religions that you must face your fear. If you go to therapists today instead of priests, they will tell you the same. Go straight to it, look it in the face. In fact, put your face right into it, the practitioners of certain Germanic tribal rites might have added. It was their custom to take a human who had been accused of cowardice to places like the Hingst Fen near Hanover and make him lie face down in waterlogged earth. They made sure he kept his gaze steady, eye to eye with the bog, by crisscrossing sticks over his body, plunging the ends deep into the mire, until he lay fastened to the bog as if by a pile of Pick-up Sticks. What to make of this? Was the guy supposed to learn something useful, to get up the next day and slosh back to the village, wringing bog water from his shirt, and tell the tribal elders he'd stared death in the face and was no longer afraid? Of course they knew he would die there. The question is, did they, in the first century A.D., also know that his body might outlast civilizations, that he might in the 1900s be unearthed, carted over soggy fens, his teeth counted, his stomach carefully rinsed, his head removed and preserved in a mixture of toluene and wax? Was he supposed to teach us, staring at his face two thousand years later, something about courage?

What we learn from the bog burials has to do with who we have been. And still are—the ways we punish thieves and murderers, our ancient need to make sacrifices to whatever brings the harvest. When we go to the Silkeborg Museum in Denmark and stare into the dark face of Tollund Man, the bog becomes an antechamber and the door is still open. What goes there in its dying might float back into the present, its face tanned and almost smiling. We may be used to the presence of the dead in cemeteries, in the leaf debris of forests, in the somber faces of daguerreotypes. We think we're on a one-way street headed away from them. But a bog is more like those rotaries I hate in Massachusetts, where you might circle for hours while other cars zoom into and out of your orbit, where whiskers on the face of a bog man brush by, your dead dog's face grins from its log frame in front of you, where you can imagine your own face unearthed from a peatbed a thousand years hence. What will they note? Your grin? Your diet of Big Macs and yogurt? The way your skin seems so real?

By afternoon, the ant is long dead, the dragonfly has disappeared, and a light rain at Cranesville has become downpour. This water will eventually slip south, tumble over Muddy Creek Falls, thrash through class 5 rapids of the Youghiogheny, and flow into the waters that drift by Pittsburgh's Three Rivers Stadium, into the Mississippi and the Gulf of Mexico. If, as some psychologists tell us, our memories are locked into the cells of our bodies, is it true for live water too? Does the river in New Orleans remember days like this when a week of rain is like a coveted hall pass in high school—permission to leave the confines of its corridors and wander to the far edge of the building where seniors with more privilege or hutzpah pool into stairwells and smooch and feel each other up, the wild abandon of brushing the hairy stems of lady slippers, fringed petals of blue gentians? I have heard people say that rivers can heal memories, but can they hold them? Can this water dribbling from a slightly tilted bowl high in the Appalachians later slip under traffic backed up on the Huey Long Bridge and disappear into the endlessness of the Gulf without losing the memory of bullfrogs bellowing from its seepy start? Can we slip through our lives without losing sight of our fingers plunged into this clogged sink of the earth, our own memories teeming with egg cases and larvae, blue damselflies and lady slippers, the smell of blueberries and decay?

Michael and I lie, belly down, on the boardwalk, face to face with that wobbly cover. Eventually we reach over and push our fingers in. We are drawn to what's below. From the safety of whatever boardwalks we have chosen, we linger at the edges, testing the mire with the tips of galoshes, a long stick, a hand. Do we dare? Do we dare? Our fingers disappear.

There's no telling what they will encounter down there or what will spy the five-pronged flesh shoved through the baroque ceiling of its world, groping around in dark rooms below. When I can push no further, it's not because my fingers have hit solid ground. What stops them is a net whose weave gets tighter and tighter the deeper you go. Down there, out of sight, my stubby fingers try tearing holes in the net, spreading apart the woof and the warp enough to push an index finger further. I can't. I'm down three inches and can go no more. I pull my fingers out, the bog slurping and slavering, and insert a pointed stick, a half inch in diameter. Standing on the edge of the boardwalk, I lean on it, pushing slowly down. I am a medieval surgeon probing the body of a patient. The stick goes down three inches, ten, twenty. Two feet down, it breaks off and I almost fall in. The water slips over its fractured tip, the sphagnum straightens, and the buried half disappears.

What's below remains, for the most part, out of sight. Cousteau's *Calypso* has yet to sail across the undulating layers of upland bog, his men stepping backward off the deck with flippered feet and high-tech, under-bog cameras to film for us *The Private Life of the Bog*. Even when Michael reaches down, grabs a chunk, and rips it up into the air and sunlight, it still isn't enough. He offers it to me. My right hand cradles it—tangled, mud-slicked roots of hair-cap and sphagnum mosses, cranberry, highbush blueberry, and wild raisin braided, twisted, and curling. But my left is wrist-deep in the swamp's sudden gouge. I am Doubting Thomas, my fingers in Christ's wound, needing to feel with my body whatever rocks and sways below the surface, whatever rises in a dream, on the verge of flooding the present again.

CHAPTER 7

Moon-White Moment

In the aquarium at Cypress Swamp Nature Center in southern Maryland, a snapping turtle is trying to squeeze through the space between the glass wall against which my nose is pressed and a cypress knee the naturalist has anchored in the mud to remind the turtle of home. It has turned its twelve-inch body sideways, belly toward me, and is paddling hard, its leathery neck tensed and stretched as it tries to squirm through the six-inch space.

It isn't the snapper itself—*Chelydra serpentina,* meaning "snakey swamp thing"—that mesmerizes. It's the color. This snapper isn't the usual mud-stained, algae-slicked brown turtle with a reputation for viciousness. It's an albino—ghost white, moon white. Rough, scaly body of antique lace, distended neck like a nubby stump of chalk. Its shell consists of rectangular blocks, each a slightly different shade of white: eggshell, marble, alabaster, ivory, and pearl. It's one of only eight documented occurrences of albinism in this species.

The naturalist and I stand in front of the aquarium watching the snapper strain and wriggle. Somebody found it in 1991, a hatchling crossing the macadam road that borders the cypress swamp. It would have been dead within days except for that rescue. "Think about it," the naturalist says, "a couple of raccoons or a fox, a coyote maybe, all roaming the woods at night, hunting for food."

I can picture the scene: all those eyes in the night and then here, across the mud, across the dark, leaf-littered ground, through the shadows of giant cypress, here comes this lumbering oval of squashed moon, fallen out of orbit, dragging itself out of the swamp.

"And there's hardly a predator in a mile who wouldn't have seen it," he reminds me. "It couldn't have lasted three days out there on its own."

And so it's been here ever since, circling in its galaxy of tank water, entertaining itself by squeezing through narrow spaces. I don't know how I feel about all this. Here's a creature, born, for whatever reasons, without camouflage, without any way of hiding. Its distinguishing characteristic is absence—absence of color, of protection, of disguise. And because it's so exposed, so vulnerable, it has spent its whole white life in an aquarium, where anyone traveling north on Route 4 in southern Maryland, as I had been, can stop for a lunch break and stand, eating a sandwich, and watch it behind its glass wall.

The naturalist leaves to answer a phone ringing somewhere, and the turtle wriggles through another inch, its curved claws raking the water. It's the shell that prevents it from just gliding through. As a child, I had imagined a turtle shell like those teak bowls you could buy at cheap import stores, a dome with some sort of straps a turtle could slip its legs through, much like putting on a sturdy life jacket. A contraption it could slip out of anytime it wanted to for a nap or an unencumbered swim. I had pictured a shell-less turtle much like a lizard, able to bask on a rock with its discarded armor nearby, able to wiggle back into the impenetrable whenever the enemy approached.

The truth is, the upper shell, or carapace, consists of a series of bony plates that are actually fused to the creature's ribs and backbone. The carapace and its counterpart on the belly—the plastron—protect it from raccoon claws, hawk talons, coyote teeth, but they're forever fastened to the turtle's body. There's no taking this fortress off. Imagine the skin on your back growing thick, fusing so completely into a crusty sweatshirt, a stiff winter jacket, that finally you cannot separate where your own body ends and this tough armor begins. There's no soaking in the tub, no scrubbing the skin into softness, no letup, no relaxing, no chancing the enemy for the feel of the sun or a lover's hand on the small of your back. You are defined by your defense. Where you go, what rain and sun and wind you feel, are determined by this shield you cannot shake off. What kind of bargain is this—this chance to live for twenty years in exchange for an armor fused to your body?

Many creatures' protective devices aren't as passive as a turtle's. The stickleback fish erects its spines; the porcupine rattles its quills. It takes less than two minutes for a chameleon to change color and vanish into its background. A cuttlefish can do it in less than a second. Even the exquisite blue gentian, rooted in wetlands, will close its flower to marauding, inefficient insects. And us? We clam up, lash out, disappear, lie, destroy. There's no finer balancing act than this: to know when to protect and when to open, when to cover and when to expose. The world can be a dangerous place, barbed and spiked, toothed and hungry, desperate to go on living. How to navigate such a minefield when the other half of the truth is that the more we shut down, the less richly we live?

This circling snapper reminds me of a man in the state hospital where I volunteered so many years ago. Gaunt and pale, he would shuffle down the corridors, flinching at the slap of rubber-soled shoes on the tile floor, the clunk of a heavy door closing. His hands would fly up, as if to cover his head. His shoulders would hunch suddenly, his neck disappearing, his face wincing away from the noise. One of the nurses told me that his body interpreted sound as invasion. Every door latching, window sliding, bedsheet billowing must have seemed to him an assault. With no way to differentiate between a harmless greeting and a red-hot poker between his eyes, he simply couldn't function in the hum and honk of the outside world. He'd been there for years, hunkered inside the shell of his ward.

And here's this albino turtle, lugging a shell, which, in addition to protecting, announces, by a startling absence of color, its vulnerability, to which we respond by encaging it. Its inability to hide makes us nervous and protective. If I woke up tomorrow, able to wander in the world utterly defenseless, would I be instantly obliterated? End up a cowering psychotic locked for life in a ward? Or a loin-clad Gandhi with a walking stick?

The albino turtle finally lurches out from between the cypress knee and the glass wall, turns belly down, and glides toward the back of the tank. Its spiny tail looks like a dinosaur's, only it too is white. And peeling, the tatters of skin trailing behind it like pale chiffon scarves.

If I could turn a fast-motion camera on any phase of life, it would be decay I'd want to see, the increasing transparency of skin and stems, human flesh growing flaky and thin, cascading from our bodies like tiny ghosts, the way the faces and breasts begin their slow sinking back into the ground. The discs between my vertebrae a stack of drying sponges. And for each of the twenty-plus years after a tubal ligation, a dozen hopeful eggs released, doomed to wander loose in my body, decaying every month while I've gone on braiding my daughter's hair, reading students' poems. I'm too oblivious to things on their way out and I want to turn this negligence around. I know that more than 90 percent of the plant world of Finzel Swamp and its surrounding woods will be eaten, not by rabbit, deer, mice, the dozens of herbivores I might watch crisscrossing this valley, but by bacteria I'll never see. The least I can do is try to imagine them. Without them, the animals couldn't keep up with disposing of the dead. Shriveled plants would clog the small channels, pile up in still pools, fill the whole valley with wet stems and damp leaves. Instead, year after year, millions of plants drop dead in the fall and by spring have completely disappeared. The Finzel valley extends north toward Pennsylvania and south toward the interstate highway cutting across western Maryland, several miles of lush wet green. It strikes me as a lot of territory entrusted to tiny mouths you need a microscope to watch. Another handspring of imagination: if I'm to stay conscious of this work they do, I have to trust again a whole world I cannot see.

In a horrifyingly beautiful book of color-enhanced microscopic photography called *Close to Nature,* a picture of one of those mouths is magnified 5,300 times. Remember in fourth grade, making those folded paper cootie-catchers whose mouths could open both up and down and sideways? Picture one made out of thin Jell-O. Picture it jawless, its shapeless, gaping, moist mouth fringed by pale green, thread-like spaghetti strands that can wave and sway and sweep water into its body. Picture hundreds of these, invisible to the eye, on the single decaying leaf that just blew onto your boot. It's October in Finzel Swamp and they have work to do. They're down there, beating their cilia in the thin film of water even a dead leaf carries.

Right off the main trail at Finzel Swamp, in the middle of a grass-green sea of thigh-high weeds, there's a clearing, maybe ten feet in diameter, where almost nothing grows. It's a circle of junk, a rusty heap of tin cans, topless radios, a russety mailbox with the flag still up. Most everything looks pretty settled here, hundreds of jagged, rust-gritty items in a pile no more than twelve inches high. If I blur my eyes and look at it, it's a foot-high collage of terra-cotta and glass, twisted coils and old wires running this way and that, like some thick iron spiderweb, an old maple syrup bottle caught in its weave, a tableau of reddish-brown grit interspersed with light, the transparency of curved glass, bits of sky, an overhead branch, a cloud moving through the junk pile. I reach with my gloved hand down through the collage and finger the most deterio-rated layer on the bottom. The shards of what used to hold green beans, dog food, artichoke hearts lie like rusted flakes of mica or corroded bark chips. I could use them for hopscotch or bingo markers, poker chips or sequins. This is what hap-pens to containers after a decades-long chemical process of deterioration.

It's not what happens to our bodies. We decay less like junk piles, more like skunk cabbage. So grotesquely humongous in April, skunk cabbages lean weakly in October against a nearby fern or lie shriveled on the ground, their edges yellow-withered and charred by a brown wind of decay, the thick, muscular stems of springtime wizened and helpless in autumn. There's just so much rot in a swamp. It's in the autumn leaves and the littered ground, spongy with the decomposed, the mud chunky with barely recognizable twig bits and leaf scrap. The top six inches of Finzel Swamp is the blended gunk of last year's growth. Stir it a bit and the trapped sulfur gasses of decay bubble out of the mud, fill the swamp with the stench of rotten eggs.

It's no wonder in the eighteenth-century American South that people were advised to leave the wet lowlands in summer for higher elevations. They believed that vapors rose up out of the swamps in hot weather like the germ-laden breath of an old man dying of influenza, like thickening mucous under the summer sun, spreading infection, slithering down the throats, depleting the vigor of any human foolish enough to be gaping at cypress knees and crocodiles. It was an understandable misperception. Miasma, they called the swamp air, meaning poisonous vapor. Today the word also suggests a funk, an aimlessness, an atmosphere in which one occasionally finds oneself, flailing helplessly, making no progress toward anything. And even after it was discovered that it was mosquitoes who breed in swamps causing the malaria (*mal*-air, bad air) that sickened so many, and not the vapor rising in some evil cloud over skunk cabbage, still the noxious reputation lingered.

Bogs and swamps still suggest the chaos of miasma, the breakdown that occurs when all the protective devices available to the human psyche collapse. Whether it's the combination of rotten egg smell and unstable ground or their ability to be two things at once, swamps and bogs have been the setting for psychic collapse for centuries, the landscape where the imagination sets its monsters loose, its frayed, ferocious creatures of shame and fear and revenge. Listen to them: the Creature of the Black Lagoon hissing, the Swamp Thing moaning, the Hound of the Baskervilles howling in the moors. Even the word "bog" sounds ominous, too much like the boogeyman my twin and I feared lurked under our childhood beds, the bugaboos, bogies, any of the bugbears and hobgoblins that can terrorize the imagination.

Bogs specialize in stimuli whose primary characteristic is to penetrate, leak through. Suddenly the skin is not strong enough and any sense of self can be lured below the surface and caught in a tangle of water lily stems, quicksand of mud, shattered by sunlight gleaming in small pools and fracturing into shadows behind hummocks. Whatever self lingers, sunlit and dry-booted, uncoils, unwinds, dissolves, seeps into a landscape of shifting dimensions. This is a valley of friable reflections where you cannot tell what is mirror, what is window, what is self, what is oblivion.

In the same state hospital where a man once flinched at every sound, I tried for several days to listen to an adolescent language-impaired child. I got lost watching his tongue. Most of us have trained our tongues well; within the caverns of closed mouths, they wait, lolling like seals on the rocks at Sea World. But let them dive into the water and they're all choreographed movement, lifting and sliding with grace, grazing the teeth, the roof of the mouth, shrinking into the upper confines of the throat, stretching, widening, a well-trained flap of muscle that does its part to move what's in the brain out of the body and into the world.

But this child's tongue had forgotten or never learned. They say that a speech-impaired child like this knows in his head the words he's trying to form, but the connection between tongue and brain has been severed. To me, mesmerized by the labored movements of his mouth and that untutored pink animal inside, it was as if his body held another language the tongue simply couldn't dance to, one that could not get out through ordinary means. What came out were muttered syllables, guttural honks, shattered consonants, the clangy rasp and rustle of half-buried tin cans, the edge-frayed skunk cabbage, and frazzled cattails of autumn. This was the deteriorated language of subterranean regions, of places overgrown with wet weeds, home to small skittish creatures, the reptilian parts of our brains scurrying about with long tails and hunger and the blind urge for sex, showing their faces only in dreams, vanishing into the recesses of mud at the first threat of daylight.

The swamp is soaked with danger—its insidious, murky, sexual wet nature always about to leak through the tight barriers of morality and hard work of anyone who goes there. For eons, artists have recognized that stage of dissolution, the firm lines of logic, brittle with rust, disintegrating, the mind a sudden blender whirring away, mashing one image against another, the dreaming self rearranging visions into slippery, glittery paradox, surreal montages of the improbable. This is the terror and truth of art, this perception of other realities, of mysteries emerging and shattering. It's a precarious world; you could go either way—into the genius of Kafka or into the terror of a honking, howling boy who wanted his wrist clenched between his teeth, night and day, because his own flesh was the only gag that muzzled the noise.

Listen to how the psychologist Erich Neumann describes the art of the insane: "Everything is still in mixture and almost inarticulated. It is almost impossible to render this phase of the world faithfully, because we are still in a formless state of creative disintegration; protoplasm, mingling decay and new birth—amorphous, atonal, disharmonious, primeval." The swamp, teeming with larvae and the decomposed, the place to go when the ordinary house will not hold the thrashings of the spirit. Here there is room for the erratic and irrational, what Rimbaud calls "an experiment in Delirium." Be forewarned. Bring some boardwalk planks, a pair of boots.

An alder leaf has a raw, jagged edge, a pointed oval some child has taken a pair of dull pinking shears to. In late summer its dull dark green takes on a yellowish-khaki hue; by now, early fall, it turns the color of burnt biscuits. The veins on the back of the leaf become more apparent, like those on an old man's hand. Smell of decay, of things past their prime, about to let go. In October, a leaf on an alder dangles by a small thread. At any moment, the cells that have pulsed all summer, sending sap and nutrients into its small veined body, will collapse and what binds it to the branch will be gone.

One time, not far from the alders at Finzel, I found a small congregation of Indian pipes sprouting out of the leaf mold. Two inches high, these albino plants resemble a sculpture of dripped wax turned upside down in the dirt. The color of breast milk, bluish, almost translucent, they are saprophytic plants, meaning they need decay in order to live. I don't know what it is about such ghostly whiteness that suggests silence, as if color were also sound and the absence of one means the absence of the other. Lovers of the damp, they don't look like pipes to me but like nuns, their heads bowed, lips open, mouthing a constant and silent syllable. If the moist ground below them could lip-read, it would see, leaning over it, a white wimpled chorus of *Oh . . . Oh . . . Oh,* the way I sometimes see the sky lean down, mouthing something, I can't tell what, when I'm lying on my back next to a swamp pool and underneath me the rotting soil answers and I know there's this giant hymn in stereo, I can feel it—in the white sky bending toward me, in the ground rotting and yielding beneath me, in the way language, old trusty bridge, fails, nicks the tongue and clatters, useless, into a junk pile, leaving me still, utterly still, until, just as unexpectedly, the spirit comes as if through the held note of a single oboe, *oh, oh,* a white shadow of music reverberating over the ground.

Year after year, I have tried to be there to watch the moment a plant died. Mostly I want to know if it falls over all at once, like a person with a massive heart attack, or whether it slowly loses its vigor, and shrinks, a man going from cane to walker to bed from which, one day, he doesn't move. I picked an Indian pipe once, brought it back to my home, and set it on a paper towel on the kitchen windowsill to watch it die. Four hours later, the head was still translucent, fleshy almost, but the bottom inch was black. By the next day, the blackness had climbed another inch. Apparently this death is not sudden or systemic, but slow and linear. It climbs the stem the way gangrene climbs a leg, the bacteria unopposed, feeding on live tissue. You'd think we could prepare, seeing death coming, climbing up our lives. The hints are all around us from the day we're born: we don't last. Our bodies are as impermanent as the Indian pipe or a tin can or our own little visions of how the world works.

Sleeping in the woods once by myself, I dreamed I was alone and burning to death in a campfire. The despair was vivid, as were the details: how the twigs beneath me glowed and twisted and burst into flame, charred flesh curling up my shins, smoke rising into the night sky. And then suddenly I was floating in outer space, nothing but cool black silence until a cool, black obelisk loomed in front of me and on top of it a white voice bloomed and whispered, *You are never alone.* I woke up in that shattery state that warns you to lie completely still until trees settle into tree-ness again, the dirt into ground, your back into the flannel inside the sleeping bag. For the rest of the night, I lay awake, listening for something that had vanished among the stars.

A second time: On a recent Friday evening, cresting the mountain above Finzel Swamp, eastbound, on the way to dinner with friends, I saw with sickening clarity that the driver of the red pickup truck cresting the mountain, westbound, was crossing into our lane, drunk, that in two or three seconds the front ends of both vehicles would crush each other, that metal would twist and char, that this could well be the end of my life. There is a kind of suspension in moments like that, something other than a slow-motion approach of the unknown. In fact, almost the opposite. It's as if whatever is so center stage in much of our lives rushes backward. That night, for about five seconds, I was suddenly aware of a vast distance between and inside all of us in that six-by-ten-foot space of Subaru, these, my friends, who'd been almost shoulder to shoulder with me the moment before, our breaths mingling in one small sphere of conversation, a sphere that ballooned in the pre-crash instant out past any visible horizon. It was as if suddenly the firmness we're used to—of our bodies, our vehicles, the asphalt beneath us—had evaporated, leaving us light and airy in slow motion, half floating in pale fog. And from somewhere in that vastness, a voice: *Pay attention! Pay attention!* I cannot explain that moment, whose voice that was, the steady instruction by which I lived through those seconds, except to say I saw this enormous space open up, and I knew I was supposed to notice, at least for a moment, that all that spaciousness was as real, as true, as the solid, dense world in which I spend most of my waking life.

It was over almost instantly, the body, with all its vulnerabilities, rushing back in, flooding the brain with messages, pain, the pure instinct of survival. What interests me now is not so much the source of that voice but the landscape of its delivery. What space is this that seems to open up only at those moments when our usual protective stances have been obliterated? Why is it we only see that space when we teeter on some precarious brink? What kind of vision don't we have? I can watch a spider, no more than an eighth of an inch, scramble over the rusted rim of a baked bean can, a sundew dissolving an ant, an Indian pipe decaying on a paper towel. Meanwhile, there are galaxies inside us, all around us, universes we can't usually hear. Does it take a dream, a near-death, a bone-deep vulnerability to sense it?

In Tibetan Buddhism, the word *shul* means the impression left when something has passed through. A cave carved out by water. A footprint in the mud. The enormous white space that opens when you stop clinging to what you think will protect you, whether it's love or success. The unguarded void that remains when you realize you're mortal, the clearing into which insight can move and some other voice can be heard. We need, it seems, some absence in order to feel the presence of something larger. Monks use the word *shul* to mean the holy path of emptiness they travel. And in Yiddish, the word means temple.

The albino snapper is scooting along the bottom of its tank, lifting its head toward the surface. I try to imagine seeing it in the wild. In the serried, mud-brown green of an Appalachian swamp, anything white appears otherworldy. One late summer day, picking blueberries at Finzel, I crouched with my bucket in a secluded, densely overhung spot. The water was dark there, almost an inky sheen, the surrounding foliage a dark gloss of green. And there, at the muddy edge, bloomed the single white flower of a water arum, its bright spathe spread like an opened ermine cloak, a ghost exposing itself to bleachers of blueberries and a single human being.

But what if it had been, not a stationary plant, but the albino snapper and you had been squatting in a wet world of mud and deep green swamp, plucking blueberries when the pure white creature emerged from black water? Imagine seeing its head first, a two-eyed, thick-necked, heavy-jawed stump of marble rising out of the inky water. Imagine its shell next, rising like a moon out of the night sky beneath you. What would you think? A ghost with a carapace? The opposite of a black hole? A drifting portal through which the world crawls out, inhales its first breath? A prophecy?

In Native American history, a white buffalo is an important omen. And since one was born some years ago on a Michigan ranch, hundreds of visitors have hung over the fences, watching her, and wondered at this news.

And on the other side of the world, in North Korea, at the sighting of an albino sea cucumber, many rejoiced and followed the bottom-feeding animal that looks exactly like its name, heralding it as a positive omen for the official rise to power of one Kim Jong Il. Imagine that sighting: you're wading or swimming in shallow water and there, scooching along the muddy bottom is a pure white cucumber. You lean over to pick it up and stand there, feet sinking in the mud, hands holding this wobbly, oblong moon.

I did just that in the mudflats of Alaska once, with an ordinary sea cucumber, which sagged in my hand like a water balloon. I'd been watching bald eagles on shore and a grizzly smacking at salmon, like scenes from *Wild America,* when this bloated, vegetable-looking thing washed by my feet. I didn't like the looks of it, but egged on by others, I leaned down and scooped it up. I didn't know then that some species of sea cucumbers, when threatened like this, will actually expel their innards through both ends of their bodies, leave a predator like me baffled by the sudden coils of entrails. The cucumber, meanwhile, suddenly dropped to the ground, will frantically extend and contract its hundreds of minuscule, fluid-filled legs and escape, gutless, to some safer place, where it spends a couple of weeks regenerating its insides. Talk about giving everything away to protect yourself! The Alaskan sea cucumber didn't do that, perhaps because I so quickly returned it to the water; nor, evidently, has the Korean creature, still floating like some tiny Moby Dick in Asian waters, heralding not disaster, but good fortune for a ruler.

Back home in Finzel Swamp, the alder leaf, otter brown, the texture of parchment, has dropped to the ground. An alder leaf curls as it dies. Its two long edges roll toward each other, the way you, lying on top of a blanket, might reach sideways, grab both edges and pull the blanket around you. Except that inside the leaf, there's nothing. The ground beneath an alder in late autumn is littered with these dark brown, empty papooses.

And here, inside the nature center at Cypress Swamp, the albino snapper is rounding the far corner of the aquarium again, its white, clawed feet combing the water, headed on a tilt for me and that tight space between the glass and a cypress knee.

I don't think any of this is about hope. It's about how closely bound are absence and presence, decay and the spirit. This, the swamp shows us, is what everything comes to—tissues and bone gone soft, the psyche thready and unraveled, skulls mushy as dead mushrooms, the invisible world munching away. And in the midst of decay, a white arum exposing itself, a moon, a plant with bowed head, white pockets of absence, these breathing, ambling, paddling shapes of blankness and vulnerability. The marble pallor of pinesaps, the white note of an oboe, the moment between death and rebirth when, according to Tibetans, "one inwardly perceives within the mind-space a vast sky full of white moonlight." A moment without artifice. Without adornment. An enormous moment—patient, unprotected, waiting to become anything.

CHAPTER 8
Clearing

The clerk in the fishing aisle of the discount sporting goods store holds my elbow steady as I lift my right leg and push it down into the long tunnel of a man's size-nine hip-wading boot. "This is the smallest size we have," he apologizes, as we watch my narrow foot disappear into three and a half feet of vulcanized rubber, bend at the ankle, and wiggle past the heel, the arch, into the semihard toe. With his help, I plunge my left leg into the other boot and practice taking small steps. It's an odd feeling—the lower half of my body completely protected and warm, ready for water, but thick-stiff and foreign, as if the bottom half of an old rubber mermaid has been sewn onto my waist and we, stitched together, have been set to lurching between the displays of fishing poles and plastic worms.

Sunday is a scheduled workday at Finzel Swamp. The Nature Conservancy has rounded up volunteers to go into the swamp from the northern, less accessible, end: they have recommended waders for the crew, just in case we encounter deep holes, unexpected plunge-throughs. I'm sure I'll be flat on my face before I even reach the edge of the water, these boots make me feel like such a clumsy, hybrid creature. Something in me resists this purchase. I practice turning on carpet, taking small clompy steps around a bin of red and white bobbers. The clerk eyes me curiously: "How do they feel?" he asks. *Like I'm balancing on a forked, finned tail,* I want to tell him. *Like I'm half fish, half human. Like I'm trying to metamorphose into some creature I'll never fully be.* I can feel a wail building inside me. All my longing to feel completely at home in the swamp comes oozing down the aisle. The carpet turns a muddy green, the fishing poles thicken into spruce trees, the stack of gear boxes softens into sphagnum. The clerk squatting on the floor by the boot box is a large frog by a stump, but I can't open or close my gill flaps and swim past him.

I'm in love with a world I can't melt into. When I go there, I have to think about my body's comfort, my ability to stay warm when there are clouds and a crisp wind and I'm knee-deep in November swamp. I don't know how to regulate my own temperature, how to grow scales on my arms, how to burrow into the mud and keep breathing. Sometimes I feel so naked and puny, so alien and paranoid about protection.

"Want to try the chest waders?" the clerk asks.

In the end, I buy the hip boots. But when Sunday comes, I leave them in the back seat of the car like a couple of discarded limbs. Our task today is to clear some brush from several sites just downwind from the swamp's small stand of larch trees. Finzel Swamp is one of the southernmost habitats for the larch, which likes wet, peaty soils and more typically grows up north in colder climates. There aren't many of them here, several dozen maybe, but they stand out in this cool November landscape. Most of the swamp is bare-sticked now, the alders and red maples, the arrowwood and hickory having dropped their leaves over the past few weeks. But the larches pose like feathery gold pyramids against a bleak backdrop. They are the only northern cone-bearing trees that drop their needles every fall, and it's as if they refuse to fade into the inconspicuousness of a deciduous winter without this late autumn finale that waits until all the black gum and maple hoopla of saffron and fire has settled to the ground.

It begins in September. The delicate, inch-long needles that have plumed the tree all summer long are still blue-green, fan-shaped clusters crowded on twigs. As the leaves of other, brighter, deciduous trees begin to color the hillsides and valleys, the needles of the larch grow pale. By October, its needles are almost invisible in the flamboyant blaze and crackle of Appalachian fall foliage. But by November, when the forest floor is damp and thick with spent decay of hickory and birch, it's the gold of the larch that remains. I can see them in the distance as we leave our parked cars, skirt the pond, and follow an old grassy road that hugs the ridge above them. A half mile below, their needles are shot through with light. Feathered, candled trees. In a dreary sea of bare trees, they look like beacons.

Once we cross the field and enter the swamp itself, it's clear my knee-high rubber boots are enough, and I'm grateful not to be careening around in waders. We slosh through thick rhododendron, through arrowwood branches twisted and torn by a berry-hunting bear. If it's a female who's been here, she may be pregnant, her hunger multiplied by the prospect of winter's litter of cubs and the absence of food when they're born. I think of how, two years ago, bear cubs had wriggled in my arms, their mother immobilized by the drug the DNR had jabsticked through her fur, how she, paralyzed, had watched me tuck her cubs inside my jacket. I study the bear scat, want to know how recently she's been here. I can't see the larches anymore—whatever perspective we had from the road up on the ridge has collapsed in the in-your-face, clawing-to-get-through thickets of the valley bottom. Twigs lash across my face; I trip in a tangle of old roots and vine.

I am just back from a month and a half in a Tibetan refugee settlement in northern India where, in the daytime, I worked with kids on poems and, at night, I tried to understand what Buddhists mean when they talk about "clear mind." It's about perspective, they say, that flash of long-distance vision, however fleeting, in the midst of our usual crowded, chaotic clinging state of mind. One night at dinner there with Thupten and Norlha, we talked about Buddhist beliefs in karma, the inexorable law of cause and effect that follows a sentient being not only within this life, but from past lives into this one and from this one into the future. From there the conversation moved to Chinese atrocities, how so much of Tibetan culture is being destroyed, how deeply the Tibetan people have suffered. I could feel my mind whirring around something I was afraid to ask. We went on eating momos and tsampa under the watchful eyes of a picture of His Holiness, the Dalai Lama. A small altar in the living room held brightly painted prayer wheels and simple metal offering bowls. Rich, red silk tapestries of Buddhist symbols—wheels, lotus, knots, and shells— hung from the walls. Finally I blurted it out. "But what if," I asked Thupten and Norlha, "all this suffering is your people's karma? What if, in a previous life, your people had committed similar ethnic cleansing, been a nation of Hitlers or something? What if this is your due?" Both of them, black-haired, high-cheeked, dressed in traditional chubas, burst out laughing. "Of course, of course!" They passed around a platter. "More momos? More rice?"

My mind momentarily cleared, a sudden wipe-clean. For a split second I saw how you could feel something, outrage and sorrow in this instance, feel it so deeply you could commit your life to alleviating the suffering, and at the same time, how you could be not so lost in your emotions that you lose perspective. How it is possible to be on the ridge and in the thicket at the exact same time.

I struggle to keep the twisted limbs from scraping my corneas. I am bent over, ducking my head, climbing through what feels like a field of bark-covered jacks some giant has tossed onto the playground while I try to not lose sight of Ken, the crew leader, who seems to know where he's going. He finally stops us. We straighten our backs, find a patch of dry ground to balance on, and notice, suddenly, the medium-sized larch about thirty feet away. It's a solitary larch, still full-needled and gold.

Between it and us are almost two dozen clumps of thickly twined shrubs, some six to ten feet high, almost all of them a tangle of woody stems. Highbush blueberry and black chokeberry, some arrowwood, all firmly sprouted and solid on soft mounds of sphagnum. They are leafless, a few blue-black remnants of the once lush berry crop dangling from twigs. I crush some in my hands. They stain my fingertips, squirt like black ink in my palm. Every poem, Frost said, begins with a lump in the throat. Not today, I think. It isn't a lump that's got me musing here, my fingers plucking these shrunken things, piling them up in my palm. It's the sense that I'm about to see something, one of those moments you can't force: you stand there, trying not to think, repeating the gesture, picking the shriveled berries, letting the body practice over and over, fingers to bush, the small tug, the squished berry, fingers back to the growing pile in the palm, waiting, waiting without agenda, for the moment of insight, for the flash that shifts the perspective, for the new vision to slice through and reshuffle the pieces. You know you're close to something, you can tell by the way the rest of the world recedes until there's only your mind, which you try to focus and empty simultaneously, remembering the best way to do this impossible task is through ritual—fingers to bush, the small tug, the squished berry . . .

Ken hands me a pair of long-handled lopping shears. He points to a thick clump and suggests I start there. "Just cut it all?!" I ask. He shows me how to get the steel jaw of the shears as close to the ground as possible, how to make the cut as horizontal as I can. I start gingerly, gently working the curved blades into the soft mound of sphagnum and fern from which the shrub has sprouted and thrived. I want to see exactly what I'm cutting, so I stop and pull the weeds away from the trunk, reinsert the loppers, try out various angles, trying to position the blades as level as I can. Finally I tighten my hands around the handles and begin to bring them together. The first second is easy, like working the handles of an old-fashioned bellows. The next second is harder; the woody trunk resists, my arm muscles strain. My impulse is to twist and yank, but I know the cleaner the cut, the better. I keep squeezing the handles toward each other. Slowly the steel blades sink through the bark and then suddenly snap together, leaving the trunk hung up in the thicket, its freshly cut end, whitish and fibered, dangling above its stump on the ground, which reminds me of an amputated bone. One cut, twenty-some to go. In just this one clump.

I look around. The others are chatting and lopping, their arms swinging together and apart in an easy rhythm. The blades of their shears make a rapid clacking; the trunks in their clumps fall like a just released fistful of Pick-Up Sticks. They haul the debris to a nearby pile and move to the next clump.

I turn back to mine. The severed bone is nestled next to a barky rope rising from the ground like the cobras that are revered in India, where artists carve them out of stone, glitter them with indigo and gold, offer them to the temples where devotees take off their shoes and bathe the serpents with milk.

I turn around, pick up my shears, and kneel beside my clump. Its collective diameter is maybe two feet, an assortment of inch-thick trunks and smaller ones. I open the jaw blades, jab them into the clump around a medium-sized cane, and squeeze hard. The cane snaps and I open the blades, jab, squeeze, open, jab. I'm trying to get rid of the severed bone and milk-bathed serpents. I'm obliterating them in a flurry of repetition, a chant of exorcism I do with my body. Jab, squeeze, open, again and again. The slashed canes collapse against each other. I straighten my arms, lock my elbows, and sever and whack, my hands on long handles pulling out, pushing in; I'm a stiff-armed spectator in continuous applause, on my knees beside a copse of chokeberry, shearing it to the ground, cane by cane.

Efficiency, I think, is inimical to an imagination in love with byways and stop signs, a closet full of costumes, forest laden with fern plumes, a detour to anywhere. This single-minded hacking drums out every metaphoric thought I've got. I'm pure physical being altering the shape of what's in front of me. I'm fast, effective, productive, momentarily aware that my canes are now dropping almost as fast as everyone else's. Gone are the images of serpent and bone. I'm getting the work done. And I keep at it, moving from one clump to the next. By now, someone has come over to haul my brush away, to keep the hewn trunks from clogging my access to the next shrub. It feels good to work like this, steadily, with a single focus fixed only on what stands a foot in front of my face.

Much of human history could be told as the history of our clearings, our impulse to clear forests for farms, swamps for cities. We seem to associate the cleared with the civilized. We clear a man of false accusations, we clear off old scores, we clear the decks and our throats. We tidy and clean. But inside, we're a mess, a yammering conglomeration of instinct and reason, reverie and logic. Maybe the impulse to clear brush, drain swamps, manicure our forests signals our discomfort with our own cluttered interiors. I'm struck, at times, many times, by the glut of long-winded chatter that goes on inside my head, the cluttered, mutating hybrids of feelings and thoughts that can whirl into a decent line of poetry or leave me stranded, speechless or gibbering drivel. I rely on Whitman to ease my fear of daffiness: "Do I contradict myself? / Very well then I contradict myself, / (I am large, I contain multitudes.)" If only we could relax, simply acknowledge our tangled and messy inconsistencies. If only we could see profusion of paradox for what it is—rich, full of possibility. It's hard; the specter of foolishness looms. We set fire to field, pick up shears, a bottle of malathion. In a clearing, interior or exterior, we can tell if we're making progress. And we like that. It's reassuring.

In contrast, in the natural world, uncomplicated by emotional gnarls, the impulse is to cover, not to clear. Left alone, the edge of a wood creeps into an abandoned field. Common ragweed, asters, and goldenrod invade. Shrubs and small trees gain a foothold, blackberry and sumac; hawthorn and spindly locust sprout along the margins, followed by birch and choke-cherries. Pretty soon a wide swath of new, sparse woodland circles the field, which begins to shrink, its tall edge grasses less robust in the now weaker, filtered sunlight.

Once, a few miles from here, I hiked down a wide streambed that leads to Savage River and found myself in the middle of nowhere in an abandoned orchard overgrown with maples and white pine. The knurly trunks of apple trees were still recognizable, their once-pruned shapes and careful distance from one another a sure sign of some long-ago cultivation. But the native forest, tall, canopied, and relentless, had years ago invaded, filled in the aisles, surrounded each tree. Locusts rose higher than the low crowns of apples, their old branches sparsely blossomed, their fragrance almost imperceptible. The whole scene reminded me of Sleeping Beauty's castle, the vines clawing up the stone walls of my childhood picture books.

In a typical boggy wetland, the process is often the same. Many bogs are actually dying lakes. What had once been wide open and filled with clear water begins to accumulate organic debris on the bottom. Grasses and reeds edge the lake's perimeter and eventually sink their roots into the shallow water. Shoreline vegetation reaches out toward the center of the lake, which grows shallower and shallower as organic sediments pile up in the bottom. Gradually, a floating bog mat creeps out over the water, tendril latching onto tendril, a whole cushion of tiny clasped hands that thickens and spreads, begins to hold soil enough for cotton grass and cranberry, which give way to red maple and black spruce. Except in the extravagant sweeping away by fire or flood, nature is relentless in its slow closing over, the world growing thick and heavy, the spongy lids eased back over the pots, the leafy curtains drawn.

I'm vaguely aware of this curtains-drawn intimacy of the hour or so I work with the thicket in my face. And its comforting familiarity. When I was eight or nine, my parents had a large, walk-in closet. I loved to go in there during the slowness of late afternoon, close the door and stand among my mother's dresses, my father's suits. In pitch blackness, I'd move around the closet, ducking under clothes poles, stepping over shoes, parting the silk blouses and wool suits, a cotton shirt-waist dress, and once, for a short while, a chiffon, full-skirted dress with a sewn-on scarf that poofed and slunk around the neckline. I'd hold the sleeve of what I knew by touch was his flannel shirt, her velvet blouse; I'd push my head into the long row of necklines and shoulder seams and move, face first, from one end of the closet to the other, through the tweed jackets and quilted bathrobe, the light fragrances and aftershaves, the lingering smell of face powder clinging to a high collar. It was like leaning into a bevy of life-sized paper dolls with curved metal hooks for heads. I didn't make up elaborate stories about these clothes in my parents' closet. What I wanted was to spend ten or fifteen minutes by myself in that small space, almost blindly gathering the cloth bodies around me, and then to open the door and step out into my parents' bedroom. It was that transition that interested me.

Theirs was an ordinary bedroom in a suburban house, bleached white furniture and eggshell walls, twin beds, a small chair for the dog near a west window the sun flooded through.

But after the closet experience, the room always looked different, new somehow, as if the furniture had shifted a bit, a window widened, a wall inched back. Always brighter of course, but also more dilated somehow. I'd study the angle where two walls met: was it still a right angle or had one wall pivoted a bit, opened up the angle just a degree or two? The beds seemed to float just an eighth inch off the floor. I sensed this not because they seemed higher but because I was sure I could pass a sheet of notebook paper under the bed legs. If I stood in the closet doorway and extended my arm, it felt as if everything was just slightly out of reach, as if I could walk toward the bed and it would slide back from me. And proportions slipped. The dressers were smaller, the chair shrunk. Most startling of all, the furniture looked suddenly so temporary, as if it had taken a deep breath and was holding it to keep its woody molecules together in the form of a dresser, a table, but that at any moment it might exhale and collapse into wood chips and sawdust. I would stand there, holding my breath, the whole room inflated and emptied of something denser, which soon enough flooded back in, settled the beds back on the floor, righted the wall angles, and left me enchanted and perplexed.

Years later, I read about a man, blind since infancy, whose sight was restored when he was in his fifties. After the operation, he could not determine size or depth. He bumped into counters and doorways and hesitated at the tops of stairways, which resembled horizontal planks with ladders on top. He could not begin to judge distances: a tree outside in the yard was no farther away than the table at the end of the hall. Perception of depth, distance, maybe even density and stability, all change when sight is restored, the curtains tied back, the closet door opened. The trick is to remember that, to know our vision shifts. I sit up in bed in the morning and sometimes I don't know if that's a blindfold against my eyes, a micrososope, a telescope. Do we ever really know what we're looking at?

Up on the high plateaus Tibetans don't cover their dead or cremate them. Instead, since firewood is scarce, they just leave the body exposed on a mountain in a ceremony called sky burial. Whether it's their soaring, cloud-skimming geography or their deeply embedded Buddhist background, my friends Thupten and Norlha know something about uncovering; they can see much farther across a spiritual landscape than I can. In exile or not, they try to live their lives in a clearing they have to keep making. They study their minds. In meditation, when a thought arises, they acknowledge it and let it go. When a feeling overwhelms, they acknowledge it and let it go. They watch things sprout; they gently pull out the roots; they toss weeds from their thinking. They can both accept that their current plight might be karmic and also know that such a cosmic perspective doesn't erase the need to clear away thorns, and it doesn't diminish their suffering. It lets them see farther and wider.

Bent over the clumps of shrubs, I'm not thinking of Tibetans or the tangle of poems, of course, or of orchards overtaken and strangled, or of my parents' bedroom closet. Though I'm vaguely aware of some familiar feeling, I'm barely thinking. I see what's in front of me. I see the many-stemmed shrub, its reddish bark and stippled twigs. I do not entertain options, debate which trunk to cut or how. I sever them all, one after another. In the back of my mind I must know that Ken will stop me if I head, shears first, toward a yellow birch, a red maple. I have no sense of bigger purpose. I have even forgotten about the larches.

Until I straighten my aching back. The rest of the crew are pulling off their work gloves and rubbing their necks. We are standing in a different place. I feel this bodily, even before I look around. Eyes closed, I know I could spread my arms and start spinning and not scrape against the thicket. I'm reminded of the book about a blind boy I read over and over when I was ten or eleven. After a firecracker accident that seared his eyes, he learned to feel the cushion of air against a wall. Arm extended, he could walk right up to it and stop just an inch away. I don't know if the air thickens against a wall or whether he could feel a certain heat or coolness or echo there, or how our bodies can sense the presence of something nearby, or in this case the absence, can know with the skin that the air is moving differently now, unobstructed.

I'm in a clearing I'd forgotten I was making. The circle is thirty feet in diameter, its circumference a push-backed ring of tangled gray thicket, hundreds of dismantled skeletons with their bones interlaced, and here again, the blue-black berries, like misshapen eyeballs, their snippets of vision still dangling from twigs. Inside, what had been obscured is now visible: a damp carpet of trampled, autumn-dead debris, its background the seal-brown softness of mud. Woven into it, buff and bronze grasses loop and splay among the flattened, sepia leaves of some creeping plant I don't recognize. Though it's muddied and tromped, the ground glistens, a readied seed bed, newly washed and spread in the sun at the feet of the larch to dry.

We have moved a wall back, opened some space in here, created what eighteenth-century philosophers called a *lucas*.

It's a word related to "lucidity" and "luminous," to the idea that light enters through an opening, whether it's a window, an eyeball, a clearing in a swamp, a bleached bedroom beyond the warm wool of a closet. It's these openings, these clearings, that early philosophers believed were the primeval sites of all our cosmologies. The absence of leafy canopy in a clearing opens a circular view of the heavens, which the early Greeks and Romans worshiped. Their most powerful gods lived in the skies, hurling lightning and driving chariots. Humans looked up to the stars and weather, to lightning and bird flights, as auguries. In Roman mythology, Vulcan burns a hole in the forest so he can see from what direction Jove's lightning bolt is hurled, so that something of the future might be foretold. The charred clearing becomes sacred ground, a burned eye for divination, a place to listen to the gods.

Here, in this new clearing, the first gold sprinkles of needle-drop litter the ground at the base of the larch. I reach up, finger the cones on its branches. They resemble tiny roses, less than an inch long, carved out of mahogany. Some of their scales, like petals, have spread, their seeds spilled. I'd like to be here on the day that happened, to sink in this soft clearing and listen for the gods while hundreds of tiny cones opened their rosewood petals and thousands of seeds, paired and long-winged, blurred the air and millions of gold needles brightened and fell from the sky.

Who knows whether any of them will make it. We've cut and hauled and cleared and opened up a space for them. In the meantime, come spring, the shrubs will send out new buds, and out of the stumps, small shoots will burst. The underbrush will grow back, thick and clogged. There's another dozen larches a few hundred yards away, plenty of minds congested and fertile, hundreds of poems yet to be started. The blue-black berries are eyeing me. *Fingers to bush, the small tug, the squished berry,* and suddenly I see it's the exuberance of growth against the process of clearing that interests me, how to hold the woolly texture of passion in the wide spaces of wisdom. It's the way I know these berry-eyeballs as metaphor, some promise of vision left dangling on these bushes, the precarious thread that keeps them from dropping, the way I can feel I might be about to see something differently. The lopped bushes and old anxieties will sprout again; I'll clear the jumbled debris from what's gold at the center of a poem and see that clearing moves me to the muddled start of the next one. "Keep walking," Rumi says, "though there's no place to get to." Keep clearing, though there's no end to resprouting. We're in this for the long haul, I think, this writing and planting, this relentless growth, this pruning and reshaping, this mind cluttered and cleared.

I wander off a bit, just to the south, to where a small pool glistens in a thicket break, another Cyclops' eye in the middle of a grizzled forehead. I look down—shimmery, bark-wrapped hieroglyphics reflected in the water—and then up— uninterrupted sky-view, Vulcan's clearing. Ken studies the bigger grove of larches to the west, suggests we pick another weekend, says we'll need hipwaders to reach them. I'll need more practice walking in them, finding some way to keep my balance. I wonder how often a Buddhist mind on the way to a clearing wobbles and sinks, whether Thupten and Norlha have their own spiritual version of boots. If I go with Ken some other weekend, I'll be clumsy and awkward, maybe fall on my face. Between here and the next clearing we'd make, a lot of woody rubble. The bears are in there, too, rummaging for last minute snacks before they hole up for winter. They're hungry and impatient. The larches glow in the afternoon sun, their roots sunk in sphagnum, their branches, gold and fili-greed in late autumn, a grove of feathery beacons.

CHAPTER 9

Remains

I find it, finally, in a corner of the seven-gravestone cemetery tucked into the woods at the edge of Finzel Swamp. Within the overgrown graveyard ringed by barbed wire, slack and tangled in the underbrush, the tombstones of "Charles Wolfe, 1825–79" and "Louisa, his wife" crumble and lean. And six feet away, next to "Liesette Franke, 1838–1914," a pile of bear scat. A good-sized pile. I kneel down and poke it with a stick. Dark brown, more smooth than gritty, more plant matter than beechnuts or fruit. It smells vaguely like the sweet ferment inside a silo. I imagine this bear's a female and wonder whether she's pregnant. She's evidently still finding food, though there are far fewer berries in this scat than there were in the droppings I'd seen down by the larches just a few weeks ago.

Today is the day after Thanksgiving, the day before deer season begins in western Maryland. Starting tomorrow, I'll stay out of the woods and swamps for a couple of weeks. In the yard, I'll put on a red plaid jacket to go out and fill birdfeeders;

I'll tie a bright orange bandana around the dog's neck even if she's right outside, carrying sticks across the driveway. But today is a gift, sandwiched between yesterday's feast and tomorrow's rifles, cleaned and loaded. For the last ten days, it's been unusually warm, and the pile of bear scat tells me what I wanted to know: that at least some bear are still out and about. I'm determined to see one before winter settles in.

I don't know how a bear anticipates her hibernation, whether she knows that soon she'll curl up in a den or under an outcropping and doze for several months. Does anything besides hunger send her lumbering across fields, down to the swamp for a few last visits? On the days before I leave for weeks in India, I slosh around Finzel, touching the rhododendron, smelling spruce needles; in my yard, I straighten logs on the woodpile. When I finally sold an old car, I stashed pennies under the floor mats, in the trunk and glove compartment. All these gestures leave some trace of myself, a sense of order or surprise, a dab of oil from my skin, anything to remind someone I've been here, touched that. When I wake up suddenly at the end of a dream, there's a similar lingering. I turn on the light, look around, study my hands for a stranger's hair, someone else's fragrance. And here's this scat among gravestones, remains and remains sinking into the ground under a thickening drizzle. Is this about saying goodbye? Or marking territory? What are any of us supposed to remember?

The leaves around the bear scat are heavy and wet. No sign of paw print, of where she headed from here. In a wilderness workshop I once attended, the teacher, a renowned tracker and storyteller, told us one of the keys to successful tracking was to be able to think like the creature we're trying to follow.

We'd spent four days with him in upstate New York, leaping through the field like a deer, crawling on hands and knees through forest like a five-toed possum, pausing to study the color and texture of raccoon scat. *Think like a bear.* She had probably come down from the ridge, headed toward whatever shriveled food was left of the blueberry crop, chokeberries, and hazelnut, even insects, under the soft bark of spruce in the swamp, anything succulent.

The trees just downhill are bare and dark, starkly outlined in the late afternoon of late autumn. Below them, the swamp is veiled in fog. I scan the valley, trying to find some marker, some buoy in this gray sea that will help guide me to the clearing where the larch tree stands, the clearing surrounded by bear-damaged arrowwood, bent alders, the dwindling food I think this animal might have headed for. Everything is obscured by fog. I point myself north, knowing only that the pond must be straight ahead, that I have to circle it and find an old road on the ridge, cross a big field and enter the swamp at just the right place to find the trail that will lead to the clearing where I think she'd find food. Rain drips off the trees. I wonder at my own willingness to walk straight into an oblivion that will erase all perspective, all sense of distance and direction. Do I think I know this swamp that well? There's a bear down there somewhere.

I head for the pond. Even when I'm sure I'm within fifty feet of it, it's still invisible. I can see only the end of the grasses, which look like the edge of a cliff, the edge of a continent. Beyond, just a blur. Pond? Wet sky? An ocean I'd forgotten was here? When I was a child, my mother painted a foggy seascape of slate grays and blues, opaque ocean blotted against the shore, thinning into a not-quite-luminous cloud that hovered low over water and beach. Some weird combination of the primordial and ethereal hanging on our living-room wall, the primitive about to become spectral. In the left foreground, a mass of marsh and dune. And behind the dune, what? Always, even as a child, I was sure something was back there, something hunkered in the sand or crawling out of the sea. Or back into. Nothing concrete in the painting suggested it, not a blurred shape or a shadow in the sand. It was more the feeling that anyone who could paint such a scene of hovering, of imminence, of the utter tenuousness of sky and sea and sand, would also see what was hidden in damp grain and fog.

I used to press my nose to those painted dunes, to try to look right through them, but of course, that close, they're not dunes anymore. They're brushed swirls of oyster and ash, smudges of wet dust, blotches of smeared eggshell. What did she know about that blurred edge between water and land? Why wouldn't she show what lurks inside it? I can't even tell whether that dark, dense something ahead is a rock or a beaver. Something plops behind me. An acorn? A paw pad?

Once when I set off on a hike in Alaska, a guide told me that if I met a grizzly on the trail, I should drop slowly to the ground, curl into a fetal position, keep my eyes averted. I found this advice unnerving. I couldn't imagine being able to adopt an infantlike pose in the presence of three-inch claws and incisor teeth. But there's something wise here: to know there are times to fight and times to submit. Tibetan Buddhists, in fact, say our whole lives are opportunities to practice nonaggression, a series of encounters with dragons, various embodiments of Mara, who tempted the Buddha with lust and greed as he sat in meditation. And, the Buddhist stories say, when we come around a turn in the path and there it is— the grizzly-dragon looming in the form of a hurtful lover, a neglectful parent, puffed-up pride, or some memory we don't want—that the secret is to sit right down on the path in front of it and practice breathing and softening, to try to see it clearly and gently, to get to know it with as much tenderness as we can muster. More unnerving advice. There's a bear out here. Could I do it?

The unexpected encounter happens, whether we're painting, building bridges, raising children, all acts of creativity that leave us exposed in uncertain territory. It happens in a poem too, where we're tracking something wild and elusive through the landscape of imagination. Often it's something that's been stalking or eluding us, waiting in the periphery of consciousness. What to do when it lands suddenly in the middle of a stanza? Cut it down to size with wit and precision? Erase it? Take a deep breath, probe it with image, tentative language, the pause of a line break?

This bear out here isn't a grizzly, but a black bear, solitary, long bellied, burly, one of the animals that resembles humans most. She can stand upright or sit on her rear; she crosses her legs, snores, sighs, and moans. She loves sweets and spanks her children. I listen in the gray nothingness for any threat sounds—huffing, grunting, teeth clicking, ground slapping. Suddenly two small rocks lift off in front of me, their wings slapping the water.

I squint into the fog and move slowly, every few steps a reassessment, a revision, the way writing a poem can feel, moving cautiously, a few halting words at a time. Not a time to sprint or leap over gullies. A time, instead, for the deliberate, word-by-word crawl. You move carefully across the pages as if any misstep would lead you forever in the wrong direction, as if one wrong word, inexact nuance, imperfect shade of berry balanced on the imperfect word for stain would cause the whole thing to collapse, an unbalanced house of words tumbling, the whole poem in disarray. It's agonizingly slow, has none of the thrill of a rushy-headlong write, and my students hate it. It's too much like work.

Next week in class, I'll tell them about the bear obscured by fog. It will be a lesson on the limitations of vision. About getting used to walking through a dim and featureless landscape. They'll squirm in their seats. Writing or walking, they want to know what that vague shape is ahead, that faint image or feeling, whether it might dense into stone or sink its teeth into their wrists. Don't we all? It's hard to keep going toward something you can't see, but that's what every poet does, sticking out one word-foot after another after another across a terrain where all the markers are obscured. I want my students to slow way down and notice everything—every barely visible valley, every etching, and every blob—including their own need to run, to be still, to get going again.

I know by the way the road is rising that the larch should be down to my left by now. I leave the road and start across the field. Its grasses are warm brown, honey-glazed, soddened by rain and fog. As before, I can see where the grasses stop, but not what's beyond. An underwater jungle of alder and bear? I stare and stare. In Galway Kinnell's poem "The Bear," the speaker finds bear scat, hunts the creature down, kills him, and crawls inside the carcass, dreaming himself into the magic of bear. He spends who knows how long in this landscape of tundra and transcendence, of lolled tongue that screeches and sings. He awakens, finally, in a haze of marshlights,

> *wondering*
> *what, anyway,*
> *was that sticky infusion, that rank flavor of blood, that poetry,*
> *by which I lived?*

The field ends; my boots sink into swamp. The trail is nowhere in sight. I'm not following scat anymore, or shredded trees, even footprints. Something's here in the muck that I want to see before snow closes over and it crawls into a den to doze and wait until spring, one glimpse to sustain me over the coming season, the weeks of deep snow and quiet. A mental photo I can haul out and study during long mornings at my desk if the poems aren't coming, if my mind is dormant and the pages blank. A reassurance I can imagine in January, when the bear, half awake, gives birth, her body warm and full of milk.

I am, like Kinnell's human-become-a-bear, following a calling I don't understand. Something carnal and mythic. An invisible, relentless calling. A *yes, do it, go.* Year after year, I get up and come to the swamp. Day after day, I sit down to write. Month after month, John Muir wandered a thousand miles, from Indiana to the Gulf of Mexico. A man I know sold his law firm, grew a gray ponytail, walks daily on the beaches of Santa Barbara. Another one took off his shoes last April and headed into Finzel Swamp. Who can explain what propels the monarchs to cross a continent, what tells the bamboo in Malaysia and Belize that after a hundred years, today is the day to bloom? There are millions of calls, a thousand summons, most likely a daily herald. We get up and go or we don't. We turn, sniffing the wind, looking for signs. The mind doesn't help. It's the body that knows, that tells me when the direction is right: heart thump and stomach churn, the warmth spreading across my chest, steady steps, the expansiveness, the way I'm in love with the world.

Or when the direction is wrong: blurred eyes, lethargy, the halting steps, snagged by hesitation, the pettiness I can sink to.

I'm just about to crawl through a clump of rhododendron when I hear the gunshot.

The fog freezes solid, a block of gray ice with a bullet splintering through it, a thousand fissures snaking above, beside, beneath me, fractals multiplying, the whole thing instantly formed and just as instantly about to shatter apart. I'm bent under one branch, straddling another, my breath stopped, paralyzed, waiting.

Once, in a small temple in village India, hundreds of bells in the inner sanctum began to ring as I stood just ten feet away. I was too transfixed to run, to even cover my ears. They clanged and gonged, always just a little off key, not quite melodious, the air so thick with their vibrations I couldn't move. I considered yelling. What could I say that would stop them? *Wait! Let me leave! I didn't mean to be here!* It went on and on, until the sound seemed to be coming from inside me, my leg bones, wrist bones, fingers clanging away against my sternum and skull, the clappers inside the bell of my body, jangling and pealing, some exhilarating mania of brass clamor climbing inside my head until I couldn't hear myself think. Which is, of course, the point.

One gunshot. It keeps echoing off the trees. There was

only a bear out here and me, and now there's a hunter. The lone larch is somewhere ahead of me. Finding it and maybe the bear means wandering through dense, slurping swamp, trying to distinguish the larch's bare branches in a foggy sky from the bare branches of maples. Or keeping my eyes fixed on the ground, looking for scat and needles among the other dead grasses. Finding it means wandering in a foggy swamp while a hunter with a rifle wanders too. Only he doesn't know I'm here. What had been a mist of pearly gray has twisted into a leaden labyrinth.

I didn't mean to be here?

Here is where I am, tangled in a rhododendron, heart pounding. I consider just lying down, keeping utterly still, hoping whoever is out there with a gun will go away. Or fleeing across the field, hollering, swinging my arms, unbear-like, undeer-like. Trying to look as completely human as I can. There's the palest bit of yellow light in the sky, as if the sun might actually break through, begin to burn off the fog. I could wait it out. Will the hunter bide time too, crouch at the edge of the field, reload the rifle and head in deeper, maybe away from me, as soon as the swamp emerges from the fog?

"Wait without hope," T. S. Eliot says, "For hope would be hope for the wrong thing." Did I come out here today too focused on bear scat and the hope of a late-autumn glimpse? Anticipating a bear and unaware of what else is slinking around me? I'm middle-aged and still working on the balance between resolve and waiting, swaying from one extreme to another, between what trackers call focused and splattered vision. If you're not concentrating on signs of animals, they say, you'll never see them. And if you're not at least half aware of what moves at the edge of your peripheral vision, you'll miss everything else. You'll stalk, fixated on that slight movement ahead in the trees, and never see the white tail in the woods to your right, the red tip on a wing to your left. Successful tracking depends, they say, on a range of attention. But attention to what? To what you're looking for. The scat, the paw print. *And* to what you're not looking for: the gnawed twig, the bent branches, the edges of hickory nuts, rougher if they've been opened by mice than by flying squirrels, the shape of a dig in fallen pine needles, the leaf nests of gray squirrels high up in deciduous trees. The small hollow bones of birds, the emptied fox skull, the gift of this very day, your own mortality. *Everything else.*

It's that range of attention that a stage magician counts on your *not* having. He's up there in his black coat and hat, doing some fancy move with his right hand and a cascade of white scarves. You're watching closely, the way he twists the scarf, turns his palm up. Meanwhile, the left hand—can you watch it too?—is sneaking around quietly, unobtrusively, planting the bouquet of flowers, stuffing the rabbit, doing the magic.

You're bent over your poem, brow furrowed, counting syllables, scanning rhythms, and out on the periphery—can you see it too?— lurks the shocking image. You're out in the fog looking for bear scat, and from somewhere nearby a gunshot blasts.

And now, two more from deeper in the swamp. Whoever it is, he's going away. A bear can hear the lock and load of a gun from fifty yards, and she's got a hundred times more nasal mucosa than I do. She's heard and smelled both of us and is long gone, taken off through mud and brush, headed, most likely, for the woods to the east. In the end, I walk back across the field. A few pink fluorescent ribbons hang limply from branches, marking wetland research sites. I find a discarded one and tie it around the brim of my hat.

Closer to the pond, the fog is lighter, gauzier, more yellow. Three ducks clatter up out of the water. Red osier dogwood emerges from the gray-brown thickets like a dull bruise. There's enough non-fogged air now to actually see the fog. It moves, like blown breath, over the valley. The smell of the swamp is strong here, hovering between sweetness and decay. I turn and walk back toward my car, down the lane that cuts through the swamp, hoping nobody would fire a gun in this direction. There's a small larch tree right by the lane. Easy to get to. I duck under rhododendron and step into mush, walk a short piece, and sit on the hummock beneath the larch, its needles strewn on sphagnum like wet bits of straw. Rumpelstiltskin would have spun this straw into gold. I'd wanted to see a bear and didn't. How do I spin this disappointment into something valuable?

One of my favorite childhood books was about a leprechaun and a rainbow and a pot of gold. The lesson appealed to my sense of purpose, the efficiency of setting goals, of being task-oriented: You'd go outside the moment the sun broke through a rainfall and look up. You'd find the place in the sky where light shattered into prisms and then you'd start walking. You'd keep your head tilted up and scanning, watching for the spot where red, orange, indigo, and violet arc into the earth and there you would find the pot of gold. It was simply a matter of tracking crimson maple tips, yellow blossoms, the jade of rice grass, gentians, and lobelia, following wherever those bands of colors led and then kneeling right there in the earth. I walked and walked. It took years of disappointment, finally abandoning the search altogether, to realize the treasure was there all along. At my feet, the larch needles lie pale against the green-bronze of sphagnum.

A half hour later, the fog is closing in again. What's farther than a hundred feet has totally disappeared: the large snags that stand like totems with their limbs chopped off at the elbows, the willow, my car. My legs, soaked to my thighs, are suddenly cold.

Visibility drops to seventy feet, fifty. If I were at sea, searching for a buoy, I'd be nervous, squinting for the sight of other boats, one ear straining for the slap of someone else's halyards against their mast. From every twig-tip of the alder beside me a drop of water dangles, globular, transparent, hundreds of lanterns waiting to be lit. The fog seeps closer, not enveloping the alder so much as merging with it, the way in movies a ghost can move through a wall. And then the moment it's *in* the wall, the wall doesn't exist. It isn't there anymore. It dematerializes, becomes part of the ghost, reassembles itself only after the spirit is gone. Except here, the ghost is vast; it's the whole sky moving in, dissolving whatever it touches, billows through. If I sit here, utterly still, it will move through me too. I'll grow less opaque; I'll thin into a cloud that hovers in a swamp. I'll vanish.

The air thickens from smoke-pearly gauze to muslin to wool; the world draws up close, drops a shroud over my head. Given the choice between nothingness and intimacy, who wouldn't huddle under the blanket with whatever or whomever we love? I'm here, only here. This moment is all there is and it's fully textured: drenched and hummocky, yielding beneath my feet. I don't know anything else. I crouch in the mud under a shroud of fog, finger the larch's gold needles, the fleshy points of skunk cabbage growing too soon in this unseasonable warmth, sphagnum moss woven of air and threads that loop and curl like question marks. They would live here easily, I think, a whole species of question marks, sinuous, open-ended, like the hoods of skunk cabbage, the pitcher plant, a cupped palm of curiosity. Almost under my foot, another pile of scat. Smaller, blacker, sprinkled throughout with short, silvery hairs. Not bear. Fox? An insect, antennae tapping like a blind man's cane, makes its slow, six-legged way over the largest turd. Small and crouched, I don't know anything. I yank the pointed hood of the skunk cabbage backward, off, and peer into the monk's cowl. There's no face in there, just a black hole where the neck should be.

The rain begins again. Somewhere out there, a hunter wades in the swamp; a bear has headed east. I tilt my head back, look up, feel the shower on my forehead like a soft facial rinse. Rivulets run down nose, over my chin, pool in the corners of my eyes. Shower turns to downpour, and I have to blink fast, faster, until I could swear this rain is *pulsing* down. Not just dropping in some continuous free-fall, but firing down in tiny percussive throbs. I try to keep my eyes open, but the proof is on my skin. Each droplet a tiny drumstick on my cheekbones, my brow, tapping its relentless, rhythmic language on my face, insistent and indecipherable. What cadence is this? What measure? What beat? I know almost nothing. I'm hollow inside, thrummed from above. Am I making this up?

A massage therapist tells me that human energy pulses at the rate of seven times a second, meaning that in that second's time, there are also six or eight pauses between pulses. And, she says, it's in those pauses, those gaps between vibrations, that spirit enters our bodies, stirs vague memory or insight, whispers intuition. I stand in a swamp in the rain, which seems to be pulsing down while my own energy vibrates seven times a second and in the in-between gaps some other kind of knowing swirls around me, waits to come in. I want to slow the whole thing down. I want those pauses to linger, stretch out before me, I want to step into the gaps of my own body, this landscape of patience and pause, this swamp of silence and clutter. Half wet, half dry, half opened, half closed, sloppily mundane, utterly spiritual, this ground that invites you to kneel, to sink to your knees in the thigh-climbing velvet of algae.

It was more than the sight of bear I was after. Something else: to walk with this longing that presses like whittled bone against my ribs, a vision that pulses just under my skin, pirouettes on the pointed tips of emerging skunk cabbage, sinks back into muck. The *Tao Te Ching* says, "The secret waits for eyes unclouded by longing." I don't think so. The longing *is* the secret. You hold it under your skin, one foot on a hummock, the other in muck that sloshes and sighs, teetering year after year between tremble and firm, clearing and veil.

Here the holes in the sieve of your mind open wider. Chunks of forgotten matter drift in. You follow a trail of remains. You get lost, disoriented, hunted. You notice your skin, how the pores themselves can open and close like millions of tiny fish mouths. What hungers in us is so large. What we feed it is so small. You lean against the sloped sides of an invisible vortex of fog, and music pours down from the sky and you kneel in the wet bulging earth, algae clinging to your skin, and you pray that at least once in your life every pore will open, that what knows no boundary between land and water will know no boundary at the edge of your body, that what lies riddled and pocked and hungry within you will fill and fill and fill.

ACKNOWLEDGMENTS

Grateful acknowledgment is due to the following publications in which some of these essays, in one form or another, first appeared: *The Yale Review, Best American Essays 1999, The Georgia Review, The Potomac Review, Orion, Audubon,* and *Organization and Environment.*

A huge thanks to Lynn Whittaker, my literary agent, who steered and buoyed me, and to Deanne Urmy, my editor at Beacon, whose eye for elegance helped polish the manuscript. Thanks, too, to the Maryland State Arts Council for financial support and to Frostburg State University, Frostburg, Maryland, for a sabbatical during which I wrote the final chapters.

And deepest gratitude to the Thursday night writing group: Brad Barkley, Jack DuBose, Mary Edgerly, Frank Fleckenstein, Michael Hughes, Keith Schlegel, Maggie Smith, and Karen Zealand. Without your support and brutal honesty, this book would not have happened. And without your friendships, my life would be less rich.

Library of Congress Cataloging-in-Publication Data

Hurd, Barbara.

Stirring the mud : on swamps, bogs, and human imagination / Barbara Hurd.

p.　cm.

ISBN 0-8070-8544-8 (hardcover : acid-free paper)

1. Swamps.　2. Bogs.　3. Mud.　I. Title.

QH87.3 .H87　2001

333.91'8'01—dc21

00-008993